ESSENCE AND PURPOSE OF YOGA

Raphael is a widely acclaimed teacher working in the *Vedanta* and Western metaphysical traditions. Founder of the Āśram Vidyā Order, he is the author of several books on the pathway of Non-duality (*advaita*) and has also translated a number of key Vedantic texts from the original Sanskrit, with the addition of his uniquely perceptive commentaries.

Essence and Purpose of Yoga

The Initiatory Pathways to the Transcendent

RAPHAEL

ELEMENT
Shaftesbury, Dorset • Rockport, Massachusetts
Brisbane, Queensland

Originally published by Edizioni Āśram Vidyā, Rome
as *Essenza e scopo dello Yoga* by Raphael in 1990

Published in Great Britain in 1996 by
Element Books Limited
Shaftesbury, Dorset SP7 8BP

Published in the USA in 1996 by
Element Books, Inc.
PO Box 830, Rockport, MA 01966

Published in Australia in 1996 by
Element Books Limited
for Jacaranda Wiley Limited
33 Park Road, Milton, Brisbane 4064

Translated by Kay McCarthy
Cover design by Max Fairbrother
Design by Roger Lightfoot
Typeset by Palimpsest Book Production Limited,
Polmont, Stirlingshire
Printed and bound in Great Britain by
J. W. Arrowsmith Ltd, Bristol

British Library Cataloguing in Publication
data available

Library of Congress Cataloging in Publication
data available

ISBN 1–85230–866–4

Contents

Many are the Ways by which to reach the goal of spiritual attainment: that love of Beauty which inebriates the poet; that devotion to the One and that cognitive ascent which represent the aspiration of the philosopher; that love and those prayers by means of which spirits full of devotion and ardour, in all their moral purity, aspire to perfection. There are the great main Ways which lead to that peak, beyond the earthly, the actual and the particular, where we can raise ourselves up into the immediate presence of the Infinite which bursts forth in all its radiance from the depths of the soul.

Plotinus

Introduction

The mind of man seeks the Unknown because his present consciousness is incomplete, conflictual. In moments of great tension he asks himself: 'When shall I find the peace, the serenity, the joy and the beauty of harmony? When shall I be happy?'

These questions, obviously, imply that the individual has neither inner happiness, nor peace or harmony. And this 'unfulfilled consciousness' causes him to strive for the attainment of integral happiness, so that the individual problems in their entirety may be solved at last.

If we recognize the fact that the human being is unhappy, fragmentary and unfulfilled, two questions may be put forward:

1. What is that peace-happiness that results in fulfilment?
2. What are the practical means of achieving it?

There is no doubt that the individual has always worked towards the attainment of happiness and of his 'existential autonomy'. Happiness constitutes a psychological aspect of enjoyment; it is an effect, and therefore presupposes an action, a movement, a relationship with those events that can produce the state of happiness.

If we look at the actions of man over the centuries we can see that he has always been motivated by the acquisition of material-sensorial things. We may say that his actions have always been of a centripetal kind, and such as to satisfy the senses and therefore the 'sensorial ego'. By acquiring, man thought he would find happiness and so solve the problem of his incompleteness. Thus, happiness has become synonymous with the enjoyment of 'something': sex, powers of any kind and level, objects, and so on. But this happiness belongs, as we have already seen, to the sphere of the egoic senses. In fact, the gratification of the senses, by its very nature, is characterized by a cyclic ebb and flow, so that even when the ego-being achieves possession it is still unhappy. Therefore, even though wealthy we may be unhappy; even though powerful we may be unhappy; even though loved we may still feel unhappy and unfulfilled.

All this shows us that this kind of sensorial-dual-egoical happiness does not constitute the fulfilment of being; it does not determine that deep peace which creates harmony. We must also recognize the fact that if such happiness is not real and constant, neither are the means-objects on which it is based. On the other hand, a non-real (relative) cause produces an equally non-real effect. We can say that all the instrument-objects upon which the happiness or unhappiness of the senses rest are harbingers of non-happiness. Only our ignorance (*avidyā*) makes us take pleasure in experiences that *potentially* constitute a source of conflict. A world of relativity contains within its deepest recesses the germ of fugacity and of unhappiness. A more thoughtful reflection helps us to recognize the fact that consciential attachment to these means-objects leads us into conflict and suffering. What is, therefore, the happiness that can make us complete? What is the happiness that will not deceive us and separate us from the true and authentic *pax profunda*?

We have seen that no means-object whatsoever, of an acquisitive and sensorial order, can lead us to the ultimate Happiness or Bliss because it is in itself a contingent and changeable instrument. How can relative and incomplete data produce invariableness and completeness? Can becoming ever be a constant? Can there ever be immobility in movement? Can there ever be stability in flowing and ebbing?

If we yearn for Bliss it is obvious that we must walk towards the sphere of the Constant, of the Unchanging and of the eternally valid. Only by taking this way shall we be able to find Fulfilment and *pax profunda*: that peace which all human beings desire and hope for.

What do the Constant, the eternally valid and

the Unchanging correspond to? Science itself offers us the answer: to the Absolute, because the relative presupposes the absolute and has a meaning only when compared to something absolute. Even Einstein's theory of relativity is based upon an absolute, upon the metrical determination of the space-time *continuum*. The constant is that which always remains identical to itself, which does not depend on anything but itself, which does not undergo any change or mutation; in other words, it is that which corresponds to the *absolute* value.

Therefore, the task of anyone who wishes to reach Happiness, with a capital 'H', is that of *discriminating*, of *discerning* and of finding the Absolute, the Unchanging, since this corresponds with the real Happiness which gives the being completeness and, therefore, peace; this, in turn, cannot but establish order, harmony and a proper relationship within the world of society. We must recognize that social disharmony is the result of the disharmony of the individual, and that if one wishes to solve the problem of the just social accord it is necessary that harmony and just accord be first of all experienced and active in the consciousness of the individual. Struggle, war, hatred and all other forms of social unfulfilment reflect the struggle of the individual with himself, of his alienation from his principal and absolute sphere, from the sphere of the Constant.

If we have understood that only the constant and absolute dimension can solve the anguishing problems of our existence, we must consider the practical means and the most suitable way towards Happiness-Bliss. These means must lead to the 'constant', because if they lead to the infra-sensorial and to the contingent and conflictual 'ego', they cannot produce everlasting Bliss. If we accept this thesis as valid we must discard many means which are normally considered valid. All that culture, that literature, that science which operate exclusively within infra-human, sensorial bounds, must be eliminated and demythicized because they cannot solve the true and pressing problem of being; rather, they increase and multiply the difficulties. The means, as we have seen, must be such as to touch – as it were – the transcendent aspect of the empirical ego; they must act as a bridge that can lead to the upper regions of being. These means belong to a sphere which is usually called the 'Sacred', in correlation to that of the infra-sensorial which is defined 'Profane'. There is no opposition between these two spheres; being polarities they dissolve into the Principle-point. They are the two ways: that of *avidyā* (metaphysical ignorance, profane point of view) and *vidyā* (Knowledge, sacred point of view).

> *They are two, hidden within the secretness of the Infinite: ignorance and Knowledge; but ignorance is perishable, Knowledge is immortal.*
>
> *Śvetāśvatara-up.*: I, v, 1

Avidyā works, in fact, within the world of the relative, the phenomenal, of movement, mirages and of the empirical self; *vidyā* is directed towards the sphere of the Principle, of the Absolute-Real, the Constant and the Eternally Valid.

Vidyā represents the initiatory Tradition of the origins, with its various eastern and western offshoots, and contains two phases of teaching: *apara,* lower or non-supreme knowledge and *para,* higher or supreme Knowledge. To the first phase (*apara*) belong those teachings which lead to the One, to the universal Seed, to *Īśvara,* to the *Brahman saguṇa* (with attributes) which pervades all, and to the one all-pervading 'substance'. To the second phase belongs the pure metaphysical Teaching which leads to the unconditioned Absolute without attributes, to the metaphysical Zero, to the *Brahman nirguṇa,* the One-without-a-second.

1

The Personal and Impersonal Aspects of the Divine

Traditional knowledge has always offered a concept of the Divine with formal attributes or qualifications (*saguṇa*) and an a-formal concept, devoid of all specific and personal attributes (*nirguṇa*). Therefore, *nirguṇa* and *saguṇa* are not two convenient formulae adopted by this or that school of philosophy or theology, but the conception of Reality itself at two levels of consciousness.

The *saguṇa* Reality corresponds with 'Our Father who art in Heaven', with Him who gives us life as creator, dispenser of grace, with Him whom we invoke, love and often fear, the creator, sustainer and transformer of all forms or life compounds, the Legislator, with Him who contains within Himself all the highest 'Qualities' that Man can conceive. In Him we move, we exist and are.

'Be perfect as your Father in Heaven is perfect'; this saying of Jesus' is the highest aspiration of those who conceive the idea of the God-Person. When we state that this God represents the One Reality, we wish to say that He is the one Seed from which all the indefinite formal conditions of the universe stem; there is nothing in the universe – no act, no event, no effect – that is not contained in this Principle-Seed. Every possible empirical truth is but a fragment of the One Truth. All worlds and entities are but 'projections' of the first Cause, and to It they return. This is a doctrine that leads all back to the Unity of Life, to the Homogeneousness of the original substance.

Empirical science has discovered that matter cannot be regarded as being composed of many different particles (the pluralistic concept), but as a homogeneous electronic mass, as energy and therefore light. We may say that science has discovered the unity of matter, while the *yogi*-philosopher has discovered the unity of life on the three levels: gross-material (the field of science), subtle and causal.

The *nirguṇa* Reality corresponds with the non-formal Principle without attributes, qualifications or determinations. It is the undifferentiated Essence from which all 'substantial appearances' spring; even the *saguṇa*-God itself is but a reflection of *Nirguṇa*. The *nirguṇa* Reality represents the Absolute without exceptions, the Unqualified, the Permanent, the Unchanging and the Constant. If the *saguṇa*

Reality is the Manifest – gross, subtle and causal – the *nirguṇa* Reality is the Non-Manifest, what is beyond the dominion of 'nature'; if the *saguṇa* Reality is Being that appears manifold, the *nirguṇa* Reality is Non-Being. This Reality, on account of its not having attributes or qualities, can be conceived only in terms of 'negation', in that in It all those denominations or causes that are peculiar to the *saguṇa* Reality are negated. Negation, thus, refers to the fact that *Nirguṇa* is unutterable. On the other hand, how could we describe something that has no relations, qualifications or attributes? Besides, description implies correlation; in fact our empirical truth is always a truth based on relations, therefore relative to something else. If *Saguṇa* represents the initial and principial Motion, *Nirguṇa* represents Non-Motion, the true 'Unmoved Mover' which sustains all.

Some might think that there are two Realities, but this would mean that duality or multiplicity are absolute, which is an absurdity; there is but one *sole Reality,* which is seen by the entities involved in the process now as *Saguṇa,* now as *Nirguṇa.* It remains the same One, only it is considered from different points of view, according to different receptive levels. We may give this analogy: matter may be considered as mass (solid) or as energy (informal); but mass and energy are expressions of one and the same Reality.

2

Bliss and the Pathways to Attain It

We have spoken about the means, ways and paths which lead to the *saguṇa* view-point and to the *nirguṇa* Reality. Now we shall examine these operative pathways more closely.

According to the traditional Vision, the human being is composed of three elements which represent a unity: body, soul and Spirit.

The Spirit is the spark connected with the Principle; the soul is the *logos*, the plastic intermediary; the body-individuality is the egoical individualized complex which expresses itself through distinctive thought.

The soul may look at the empirical, phenomenal, apparent and fleeting world, and it may look at the world of the Spirit. It can, therefore, either dissipate its energies upon the plane of objectivity and of differentiation, or it can concentrate upon itself and return within its deepest, innermost essence and there attain the Spirit, therefore God, who is the unutterable bliss and joy (*ānanda*). The return to Unity is achieved by means of freedom and of liberation from the phenomenal and corporeal empiricism.

Individuality is a reflection of the soul, and the soul is a reflection of the Spirit. The reflection of the soul's consciousness by 'descending' becomes metallized, earthly, altering its universal qualities: therefore, for egoical individuality, love becomes sensual desire to possess, or love of oneself; the spiritual, universal will to be becomes self-affirmation, self-assertion, while the noumenal, synthetic knowledge fades into distinctive, empirical, selective or differentiated thought.

Therefore, individuality expresses itself through will, sentiment-emotion and knowledge: these are three supports from which one may depart in order to enter into contact with the soul and then the Spirit.

Rāja-yoga, Bhakti-yoga and *Jñāna-yoga* found their *sādhanā* upon these three elements: *Rāja* upon will, *Bhakti* upon feeling and *Jñāna* upon knowledge. Every individual, though he can manifest himself with all or part of these three elements, has a dominant note; some are centred in the plane of knowledge, others in that of feeling, and others in that of will.

Beside these three basic types of *yoga* there are also: *Mantra-yoga* for those who are particularly sensitive to sound (although this is used in almost every type of *yoga*); *Haṭha-yoga* for those who are focused in the physical and vital body; *Tantra-yoga* for those attracted by dynamic universal energy (*śakti*), and so on.

It should be pointed out that the aim of every kind of *yoga* is the union with the Principle, the freedom of the soul from the bonds of phenomenal individuality and its reintegration with the Spirit; this involves the realization of the total, complete being. The being is Spirit and as such it must realize itself. *Yoga* is a practical discipline although it has its own philosophy. It is not a technicality confined only to the sphere of the individuality; it is not a technique for solving psychological conflicts; it is not simply a means by which to attain peace of mind or the improvement of mental and bodily health. It is a 'raft' which, if employed wisely, carries the soul from the unreal to the real, from death to immortality, from darkness to light.

If Man, as a consequence of an act of free will, has separated himself from the universal context, weakening his link with the Father, the Principle, God, the One, according to the various terminologies *yoga* is the instrument by which he can repair the break or reverse the 'fall'. If *yoga* disregards this aim, then it is not true *yoga*.

The aim of *yoga* is to lead the soul that is in us back

to the divine Soul – as Plotinus states – whereas to practise physical exercise to keep the body fit or to simply talk theories about the *yoga* philosophy does not mean practising *yoga*. To practise *yoga* we must thirst for Liberation, aspire to reach our divine counterpart, feel that *Eros* (thirst or desire for the Intelligible) of which Plato speaks. Without these the practice of *yoga* becomes a mere parody.

Unless a particular brotherhood arrogates to itself the exclusive right to possess the doctrine and the practice by which to reach God, one may accept *yoga* and practise it even in the cultural and religious context within which one lives normally. *Yoga* is a spiritual science which can be followed by anyone who remains free from prejudice and from dogmatic fanaticism.

Describing the various types of *yoga* is an arduous task because the topic is so very vast and because true *yoga*, being *living experience*, cannot be described in writing. However, by way of illustration one may touch upon some of them.

'Many are the Ways,' says Plotinus, 'by which to reach the goal of spiritual attainment: that love of Beauty which inebriates the poet; that devotion to the One and that cognitive ascent which represent the aspiration of the philosopher; that love and those prayers by means of which spirits full of devotion and ardour, in all their moral purity, aspire to perfection. There are the great main Ways which lead to that peak, beyond the earthly, the actual and the particular, where we can raise ourselves up into the immediate presence of the Infinite which bursts forth in all its radiance from the depths of the soul.'

It is believed that the *Vedas* consider three solutive phases which refer to action, worship and knowledge. The various kinds of *yoga* keep in mind these three ways by which to approach the Divinity. On the other hand it is necessary to consider the fact that the modalities of knowledge, will and sentiment (reflection, activity, emotiveness) cannot be separated from the context of our consciousness; they are but phases of a sole process and mobile aspects of an only reality: the individual.

The ultimate essence of *yoga* is the contact and the union between the individual consciousness and the divine consciousness. The human being is a divided, fragmentary entity; it expresses only a minimum part of its entire consciential cord; its nature is universal and cosmic but in its illusory self-centredness it remains individual and particular. If we take a look at the various types of *yoga* we can notice that they start from the first step of the stairway – which involves training the physical body – and arrive at the top where they touch the *mens informalis*, or the sight of pure reason.

Thus, *Haṭha-yoga* uses the body and the physical functions as instruments of perfection and realization.

Bhakti-yoga chooses the emotional body and renders

it increasingly more plastic and full of love for the Beloved until it causes the breaking of the ego level which is necessary to achieve Union.

Rāja-yoga involves the mind and all its many qualifications and movements; above all it avails of will. Creating a centre of consciousness as its lever, it gives rise to a process of co-ordination, integration, domination, transmutation and transcendence of the individualized imprisoning energies so as to burn all those obstacles which prevent *kaivalya*, the realization of the Self or the liberation from *avidyā*.

Karma-yoga takes action as the support of ascesis and, by making it a perfect act of donation, shatters the centripetal egocentrism of the 'shadow' which manifests itself in the world of *saṁsāra* (becoming). By means of righteous and just action and by abandoning the fruits of action, the individual transcends itself.

Jñāna-yoga avails of the intellect at the highest level and, by means of discernment (*viveka*) carried out by using intellectual reflection (*vicāra*), manages to distinguish what is Reality from what is not Reality. It is a procedure of selection and synthesis; by discerning absolute values in a way which becomes all the while clearer, the consciousness raises itself up from the particular to the universal, from differentiation to the Undifferentiated.

Asparśa-yoga (*asparśa* means 'non-contact', 'without support') directs its *sādhanā* directly towards the Absolute, the Unconditioned and, by insisting upon the absoluteness of Being, it urges the consciousness of the disciple to cling directly to the eternal Constant without birth, without cause, effect and change. The condition required by this kind of *yoga* is to take – without hesitation and by means of a truly remarkable act of courage – an immediate flight towards the 'without-time-space-causality', and to remain firmly rooted in it without 'descending' into the sphere of the manifest.

This is the *yoga* of the 'thunderbolt': either the consciousness anchors itself firmly until Identity is attained, or it is thrown back upon the plane of the conceptualized and of the deforming phenomenal. This is the 'Way of Fire' which reduces *māyā* with all its products to ashes in a flash. It is the *yoga* without support because, unlike the other kinds of *yoga* which base their *sādhanā* now upon emotion, now on the will, now on the discriminating mind or the physical body, and so on, this one does not rely upon either intrinsic or extrinsic qualitative factors. In this case one must grasp directly, by means of a total and complete transformation of oneself, the sense of the Absolute, of the metaphysical Zero, of the Unqualified (*nirguṇa*); this implies *finding oneself*, not projecting an image of oneself.

This *yoga* teaches us that 'by going on . . . one never arrives', by desiring one never ceases to desire; by conceptualizing now one thing, now another, the mind never attains silence; by resting upon the expressive qualities of *māyā* one never escapes *māyā*; therefore, whoever wishes to 'stop' must cease 'walking', whoever wishes to break the chains of desire must cease desiring, whoever wishes to achieve mental silence must stop thinking and whoever wishes to escape the bondage of *māyā* must not be dazzled by its products, however refined they may appear to be.

Asparśa-yoga allows no ambiguity, nor does it linger to consider the time factor (and therefore history and evolution) in all its dynamics, because the Without-time cannot be achieved in time or with time.

Evolution does not lead to the Absolute and to the Constant, but to *saṁsāra* itself. The Absolute cannot depend upon stages and phases of evolution, therefore upon spatial-temporal conditions; the Absolute *is*, and only whosoever has the strength, the power and the heroic will to Be discovers that he is Being; only whosoever dares to *find himself* Totality discovers that he *is* Totality.[1]

[1] For further details cp. *Pathway of Non-daulity* (chapter *Ajāti Vēda* and *Asparśa Vāda*) and *Tat Tuanasi – That Thou Art* by Raphael. English translation by Motilal Banarsidass, Delhi, 1992.

3

The Yoga Ethics

Because *Yoga* is neither a religion (in the accepted sense of the term) nor a unilateral creed belonging exclusively to some eastern members or groups of people, it risks being considered, especially in the West, devoid of ethics and even of a 'vision' or philosophy, whether it be spiritual or initiatory. Nothing could be further from the truth. *Yoga,* as a spiritual discipline, is contained in the *Vedas* and in the *Upaniṣads;* besides it is also one of the six *darśanas* ('points of view' in relation to the *Vedas*) upon which most of the other types of *yoga* are based. *Yoga* therefore has its roots in a deeply spiritual terrain, that of the *Vedas-Upaniṣads-darśanas*. If this very important point was not considered, *yoga* would become a mere physical or mental exercise.

We have spoken about conflict, pain, the personal

and the impersonal Divinity, *avidyā* or ignorance which concerns the nature of Being, and of *vidyā* or knowledge which reveals Being. These ideas form the base upon which all kinds of *yoga* practice must rest.

A serious and well-versed disciple, when asked why he practises *yoga,* would certainly answer in this manner: 'Because I recognize – as the *Vedas,* the *Upaniṣads* as well as western Initiatory Tradition state – the fact that I fell into *avidyā* and thus forgot my true nature; by practising *yoga* I can defeat *avidyā* and regenerate myself in my pure essence or pure consciousness.'

Plato too says that the Soul, by entering into generation and by identifying with it (Patañjali, in his *Yoga-sūtras,* states that the cause of slavery is the union between the Seer-soul and the seen-world of generation, II, 17, 18), has forgotten its intelligible or noetic nature. This divine Master indicates Dialectics as the supreme instrument of resolution; the *Upaniṣads* indicate various means, of which one is in fact *yoga.*

Therefore, in order to practise *yoga,* five factors are fundamental:

1. Aspiration towards the Divine, the suprasensible.
2. A vocation for one of the *yoga* types.
3. Knowledge of the *yoga* philosophical vision.
4. Psychological-consciential qualification.
5. Practice of the *yoga* ethics.

Ethics involve a way of behaviour, the practical attitude adopted by the individual in his everyday living. We can say that it is by a person's ethics that we can recognize his cultural, spiritual and aspiration level. Everyone has a set of ethical values, even those who think they have none.

Yoga points out two preliminary ethical aspects before engaging in the *yoga* practice proper and in meditation. They are *yama* (self-restraint) and *niyama* (observance). *Yama* includes forbearance from violence, falseness, theft, incontinence and greed; *niyama* includes purity, contentment-acceptance, austerity-discipline, study of oneself and of the *yoga* doctrine, and abandonment or rendering oneself open to the Divine.

To account for these ethical characteristics and their usefulness – and in fact their absolute necessity – a separate treatise would be required, also because they include some technical aspects of *sādhanā* (*yoga* training). It is sufficient to recall that certain *āsanas*, concentration upon specific *cakras*, or meditation (*dhyāna*) produce the emergence of energies that often the *sādhaka* (disciple) is unable to control, thus providing strength for all that is weak, impure, discordant, producing an over-individualistic psychological quality (*guṇa*).

With *yoga* a disciple may find himself in the paradoxical situation of seeking peace, calm, serenity and suprasensible bliss, and ending up instead with a surplus of energy that he can neither understand nor direct; or he may enter into a state of profound conflict, because while on the one hand he aspires towards the Divine, on the other he does not follow the ethics required by his purpose, so causing a clash and a conflict of energies of unforeseeable consequences.

Let us say that to practise *yoga,* like being a priest, a doctor, an engineer or a craftsman, requires *being qualified;* one must have specific qualifications or certain attitudes, otherwise there will be bad or false *yogis,* doctors, priests, and so on.

Sometimes it happens, and particularly in the West, that *yoga* is taken to be a mere physical or mental exercise used to attain simple psychological comfort when life has reached a level of pathological stress. But *yoga* – in its various forms – is a means by which, if practised honestly and with the right vocation, the soul can attain the Soul Divine.

4

Haṭha-yoga

Haṭha-yoga is based on the principle that the vital mechanism is sustained by two currents of energy: one is positive – *ha;* the other negative – *ṭha.*

These are the two powers, the solar and the lunar, *iḍā* and *piṇgalā,* which, when balanced, render the vital complex harmonious and make it work perfectly. The energy balance that nature itself gives the individual is held to be insufficient by *Haṭha yoga,* and therefore it tries to establish a new balance capable of permitting the physical form to bear a growing dynamic flow of vital energy (*prāṇa*), which is available in an unlimited quantity in space.

Every individual possesses a certain quantity of pranic energy which makes up his energy patrimony; or rather, every individual absorbs – by means of particular pranic centres – a quantity of energy in proportion to his receiving magnet. For example, someone may be able to resist a certain number of electric volts, but once this threshold is passed the excessive electrical vibrations transmitted to his body cells may cause him to die. But *Haṭha-yoga* opens the door to the universalization of the individual vitality and allows it to receive a less rationed flow of pranic energy and therefore one of greater and superior intensity than the normal level accumulated by the receiving magnet.

Haṭha-yoga, rather than a philosophy or a doctrine, is a method, a psycho-physical discipline which is mainly based upon two highly efficacious instruments: *āsanas* and *prāṇāyāma*. The *āsanas* are the 'positions' of the body, studied to favour particular energy flows; they also render the body immobile by means of 'control' and 'power'. The power of physical immobility in the *Haṭha-yoga* is as important as the power of immobility or suspension of the *vṛttis* (thought modifications) in *Rāja-yoga*. It must be pointed out that immobility does not imply physical or mental 'passivity'; in this particular state the consciousness is more open, ready, attentive and less dispersive. Our mind's activity is directed towards agitated, disorderly movements, capable of wasting emotional-mental energy even when occupied with futile questions. Whoever is master of his own thoughts uses up only about one third of the energy that is usually employed by an individual who does not control his mind. The waste of *prāṇa* energy during everyday living is enormous; this energy should be made available to overcome particular circumstances such as illness. Inability to stabilize the flow of pranic energy brings about an imbalance between ingoing and outgoing currents, between centrifugal action that goes outwards from the centre of the individual, and centripetal action which operates from the external towards the individual. Once this balance has been upset, the energetic state becomes precarious and although the receiving and transmitting magnet continuously tries to restore the balance, it is conditioned by this imbalance which can often cause its deterioration.

The *prāṇāyāma* (control of breathing) concerns mastery over the vital forces; in fact, breathing is connected with pranic energy, although only indirectly. According to *Haṭha-yoga, prāṇāyāma* plays a double role: on the one hand it harmonizes pranic input and output, gives greater vitality to cell tissues, and strengthens the physique to an exceptional degree, even overcoming its natural capacities; on the other hand, it favours the awakening of *kuṇḍalinī* (the *prāṇa* dynamism coiled up inside the centre or *cakra* at the base of the spine), thus revealing to the aspirant unusual and extraordinary fields of consciousness.

Some of the results obtained may take the form of what are usually called *siddhis* (psychic powers), but these do not give true Liberation or Realization.[1] These belong to the phenomenal world and in the long run may even enslave. The problem of being invests far deeper levels of awareness and requires that the neophyte aspire to more *sacred* and more spiritual goals. A *samādhi* is an experience of the universal order which *Haṭha-yoga* – if carried out with intelligence and under the guidance of a proper instructor – can offer in a prodigious manner.

In any case, the authentic *Haṭha-yoga* aims at merging, by means of the raising of *kuṇḍalinī, Śakti* with *Śiva* (the *cakras* of the base and of the head) and then from there take flight towards the transcendent state of being.

[1] With reference to psychic powers see the chapter entitled 'The siddhis' in *Pathway of Non-duality* by Raphael, op. cit.

5

Karma-yoga

Karma-yoga is the pathway of 'action without action' or of detachment from the fruit of action. This means determining oneself through an act of pure action without attachment. The average individual acts because of a desire to possess; the disciple of this pathway acts without any desire to receive. This is the *yoga* of pure action (*karma*) taught by the *Bhagavad-gītā*.

> Oh Anagha [Arjuna], as I said to you before, in this world there is a double path: that which refers to the *Sāṁkhya-yoga* by means of knowledge (*jñāna*) and that which refers to *Karma-yoga* by means of action.
>
> It is not by refusing action that man can reach liberation from action, nor is it by means of simple

> renunciation [of all acting] that he can reach the perfection of *samādhi*.
>
> Nor can anyone, even for an instant, remain without acting, because he is inevitably obliged to act by the qualities (*guṇas*) of *prakṛti*.
>
> Whoever, even by dominating the organs of action (*karmendriya*), goes on thinking of the objects of the senses may be called a dupe and a hypocrite.
>
> Whoever, on the other hand, oh Arjuna, bridling the senses and without attachment takes up *Karma-yoga*, by means of the faculties of action, shall triumph over [others].
>
> Carry out, therefore, the proper action, because acting is better than inactivity [inertia]; without action it is not even possible to make your body survive.
>
> Apart from action based upon sacrifice [non-binding action] the world is bound to action, oh Kaunteya, therefore, carry out action as a sacrificial function, free from attachment.
>
> *Bhagavad-gītā*, III 3–9

The action spoken of here is neither moved by the individual sphere, nor directed towards the individual or the particular. The disciple of this kind of *yoga* lets his individual empirical self with all its possessive and greedy tendencies die, and connects himself with the Principle for universal purposes. This is the *yoga* for people of action. Thus, the disciple becomes the instrument of divine will, favouring the process of becoming, understanding its pace and its operative modalities.

Kṛṣṇa, in the *Gītā,* continually exhorts his disciple to take refuge in him, to unite with him, to find his identity in him; and his insistence is, without any doubt, necessary in that the action of the *Karma-yoga* requires that redeeming urge of total dedication, of loyalty and devotion to the will of the universal Being; in fighting for the ideal and the just cause, the candidate achieves the breaking of the ego level with an impetus of sacrifice and immolation, where the *jñāni* achieves the same result through discrimination, discernment and intellectual reflection. In the first case there is a thrust from below, in the latter an intuitive recognition of what one really is. In the former there is action and fire; in the latter silence and contemplation full of revealing sounds.

'*Karma-yoga,* therefore, is a system of ethics and religion,' writes Vivekānanda in his work *Karma-yoga,* 'intended to attain freedom through unselfishness, and by good works. The *karma-yogi* need not believe in any doctrine whatever. He may not believe even in God, may not ask himself what his soul is, not think of any metaphysical speculation. His essential goal is to free himself from egoism and this he must realize for himself. Every moment of his life must be realization, because he has to solve by mere work, without the help of doctrine or theory, the very same problem to which the *jñāni* applies his reason and inspiration, and the *bhakta* his love . . .

'The universe might well go on forever, but our goal is freedom, our goal is unselfishness: and according to *Karma-yoga*, the goal is to be reached through work . . .

'"To work you have the right but not to the fruits thereof." Man can train himself to know and to practise this teaching, says *Karma-yoga*. When the idea of doing good has become a part of his very being, then he will not seek for any motive outside. Let us do good because it is good to do good; he who does good work even in order to get to heaven binds himself down, says the *Karma-yogi*. Any work that is done with the least selfish motive, instead of making us free forges one more chain for our feet. So the only way is to give up all the fruits of work, to be unattached to them . . . When a man can do that, he will be a Buddha, and out of him will come the power to work in such a manner as to transform the world. This man represents the very highest ideal of *Karma-yoga*.'

We must understand that Motion which does not require motion, that Action which does not require action, as we must understand that Love which does not demand Love. Can Love desire love if it itself is love? Can the Sun want light if it is light itself?

When we express ourselves as action without attraction and attachment, the egoistic self dissolves and pure Action, pure Motion, pure Being, pure Love remain.

The West, with its frantic urge to operate, its tendency towards extroversion and its continuous 'doing', ought to practise this healthy type of *yoga*. The relationships between individuals, and between nations, would soon change, creating, at last, harmony. The psychological and physical attitude of Non-violence is an essential characteristic of *Karma-yoga*.[1]

[1] For a deeper study of *Karma-yoga* see the *Bhagavad-gītā* translated from the Sanskrit and commented by Raphael, Edizioni Aśram Vidyā, Rome 1981.

6

Bhakti-yoga

The *yoga* of Devotion and of Love operates above the physical level – upon which *Haṭha-yoga* stands – on that of emotions or of feeling. This is the *yoga* that is practised with the heart, with a transmuted sentiment, with a firm and constant devotion to the God-Person. We can say that this is the most frequently followed pathway. The principle of *Bhakti-yoga* is that of utilizing the usual life ties, characterized by the play of the emotions, to 'come into possession' of the Beloved. Meditation and the ritual acts themselves are used simply to increase the intensity of the divine contact.

The individual has always turned to God to prostrate himself and ask for help. It is a natural human need to want to be protected, to *abandon oneself* to the Power of the Divinity in order to feel complete. The Sanskrit word *bhakti* comes from the root *bhj* which means 'render honour', 'cult', 'service', therefore placing oneself at the service of the Divinity with total dedication and abnegation. The disciple who experiences this 'approach' to the Divine broadens his feelings until he *feels* the Divinity within himself. These people feel love for God to such a degree that they turn their backs upon all worldly attractions. Only love and a great devotion to the Beloved can shake these disciples, possessed by divine Fury. Their immense capacity of 'becoming absorbed' is such that the Master, the Instructor or the cosmic Beloved become the Object of a deep, tenacious adoration. The disciple adores his own Instructor, his Soul (inner Instructor), the divine Instructor, according to his level of awareness. As the pathway is travelled, individuality loses all content and meaning. For Him, for the divine Beloved, everything can perish: even life if necessary.

'To the defenders of the devotional method,' says Radhakrishnan, 'it is not so much supermundane redemption that counts as absolute submission to the unchanging Will of God.'

For Love of the Father the devotees can love all that the Father loves: 'Father, not my will but thy Will be done.' It is this great thirst for devotion that spurs them up to the greatest heights of aspiration, so that their internal fires produce a great flame which raises their consciousness up into the realm of boundless divine ecstasy. Consummation is possession of God; the total abnegation of themselves makes the Divine emerge. God operates in them because they offer themselves totally to Him. The groom or bride of the Lord of Love raises himself or herself up to produce that heavenly marriage that is the tangible sign of the loss of individuality.

'He speaks to me and tells me I am his. My Lord, my Christ, you are mine, I am yours. You are my life. This heart, this mind, this Soul I depose at your feet. I love you, I love you!' This is the cry of a great *bhakta*!

And in the *Bhāgavata* we read: 'Before knowledge can arise, the fact of finding oneself within duality can be deceptive, but when our mind is cleared we can become aware that duality is more beautiful than non-duality and that it exists so that an act of cult may be performed . . . Truth is non-duality, but duality exists in order that the cult may exist; therefore the cult itself is a hundred times greater than liberation.'

The *bhakta* is he who, with deep devotion, tenderness, pity, love and compassion 'submits' to the Lord. Only unconditioned donation to the Beloved can guarantee that He takes care of the lover.

Madhusūdana defines *bhakti* as that condition of the spirit where the spirit itself, overpowered by the ecstasy of love, assumes the form of the Divinity.

If in the other paths one believes that it is Man with an act of will who raises himself up to the divine, so that there is an 'Ascent', in the case of *Bhakti,* on the contrary, God must descend into the human being, and therefore there is a 'Descent'. The individual has to empty himself of all psychological content so that the Lord may descend and save him through grace.

Bhakti is divided into *aparabhakti* and *parabhakti*: lesser and higher, non-supreme and supreme. *Aparabhakti* is concerned with the 'Lesser Mysteries' and works upon the plane of purification, of activation of ethical qualities, of psychological harmonization, and so on. *Parabhakti* operates upon the plane of the transfiguration of oneself so as to reach the 'perfection of the Father' and identify with Him.

It might be said that *aparabhakti* is exoteric, while *parabhakti* is esoteric; the former reveals itself at the individual, particular and general level, the latter on the universal, noetic plane, on the plane of the Principle. We may also say that the former is concerned with asceticism, the latter with pure mysticism.

The term *bhakti* means participation, devotion and donation, and donation-devotion is achieved through Love (*prema*). *Bhakti* is therefore the gift of oneself to the Father for Love.

> God is Love: whoever loves is in God, and God is in him.
>
> I John: IV, 16

Like all other kinds of ascesis, it has its phases, its

operative modes and its perspectives. As *yoga* is of a practical order, the only thing one can do is to point out a precise and definite *sādhanā* (ascesis).

In order to facilitate the western Christian, we are presenting the *sādhanā* of the *Prema-yoga,* the *yoga* of Love. This kind of *sādhanā,* however, disregards Christian theological postulations and we apologize if something is not in agreement with such postulations. For obvious reasons we must outline the general principles which inform this *sādhanā*.

In the world of Eden (*brahmaloka* for the Hindus) there are the Tree of Life (Unity), and of the polar, good-evil knowledge (becoming or *saṁsāra* in Buddhism). Primordial Adam, through an act of free will, tastes the fruit of enchaining dualism and in order to free himself he must *find himself* again and achieve identity with the Tree of Life or Truth.

Christ came to give us 'the keys to the Kingdom of Heaven', that is the 'freeing' teaching. In the *Gospel* we read:

> Then the disciples came and said to him: 'Why do you speak to them in parables?' And he answered them: 'To you it has been given to know the secrets of the Kingdom of Heaven, but to them it has not been given.'
>
> Matthew: XIII, 10–11

Jesus incarnated the Principle of Love which is consubstantial to the Father. 'No one shall go to the Father except through me.' Christ is the Son of the Father because Love, with Will and Knowledge, is consubstantial to God.

In the East they speak of Brahmā, Viṣṇu and Śiva and these may be compared with these three aspects which in turn may be called the Father, the Son and the Holy Spirit.

Love is therefore the key to open the door that was closed when Man chose to experience imprisoning dualism (the Tree of good and evil).

When the polar extroverted desire turns into unifying Love for the Tree of Life, then Adam goes back to being pure undivided Spirit.

If original sin or the 'fall' caused a separation between Man and God or placed them at a great distance, the Love-Son, born of the universal Father-Mary, covers that distance until it is annulled. Love is the opposite of egoism, and egoism caused the separation.[1]

Refusal of Unity and attachment to multiplicity, particularity and individuality caused Adam to cut himself off from the Whole (God) and set himself up as a single element among single elements, in opposition to the Principle. The *Vedānta* states that the degeneration of *buddhi* led to *ahaṁkāra*, that is to the sense of ego or to egocentredness.

Christ 'anchored' onto the earth a universal Principle which must be grasped, assimilated, lived and expressed by the fallen Adam who wishes to return to the 'primordial state'.

Love may be interpreted in either esoteric or exoteric terms, and according to the point of view adopted to consider it, the vision changes.

In general, humanity has always interpreted Love in terms of egotistical sentiment, of *desire*, while Love (and it is worth insisting on this point) is a universal Principle, like Will and Intelligence. By humanizing and anthropomorphizing the God-Christ men have brought this principle down to the simple level of emotional feeling; it is well known that emotion, being above all a characteristic of the ego, seeks gratification and psychological comfort.

A philosophy, a religion, a political concept, and so on, may be created to satisfy the ego, to comfort it rather than to solve and transcend it.

INITIATION INTO THE MYSTERIES OF LOVE

The '*Yoga* of Love' (*Prema-yoga*) comprises five stages or *aṅgas*, which were expressed by Christ himself:

Baptism-Purification
Transfiguration
Crucifixion, or 'death' of the ego-individuality
Ascension
Union

These phases which Christ went through may be

interpreted at *apara* or at *para* level, from the exoteric or the esoteric point of view. *Prema-yoga* regards the *para-bhakti* level. It may be worth remembering that these five *aṅgas* can be correlated with Patañjali's eight *Rāja-yoga* means.

The first two stages lead up to the death of the ego, born by experiencing the Tree of good and evil. Purification involves elimination of all the dissonances that obscure and veil the vibration of the Love-Principle; Love which has always been resounding because it represents the Father himself, but which the fallen Adam has transformed into something inferior and distorted, into desire and into love of oneself. Therefore, it is necessary to find the original vibration again: this implies tuning into that primordial Sound which makes 'the sun and all other stars move'.

After the purification or 'baptism by fire' (thus defined because with it all the impurities within the psycho-physical context are burnt) comes the transfiguration which changes individuality, cleanses it, renders it completely innocent and *luminous* (and this is not meant in a symbolical sense).

This consciential state, profoundly oriented towards the glory of the Principle, leads to the crucifixion or *death* of the entire egoistic-individual complex; the Adamic nature, patiently nourished, is broken and in the desert without projections and without any kind of support, the consciousness hears the sound of Love which grasps, attracts, and sublimates.

'Nobody is rich in God if he is not entirely dead to himself,' says Meister Eckhart.

> Father, into thy hands I commit my spirit.
>
> Luke: XXIII, 46

Ascension is *flying* – because one is made light by the previous phases – towards living Love as essential Reality: 'It is no longer I who live, but it is Christ who lives in me.' It represents the rapture of the lover for the Beloved, the realization of heavenly marriage; consciousness brings itself closer and closer to the very source of Love up to the point of union. In such an ocean of joyful, ecstatic Love, it produces identity with the Word.

> I and the Father are one . . . Whoever sees me sees the Father . . . and the glory that you gave me I have given to them, so that they may become one thing just as you and I are one thing; I in them and you in me so that they be perfect in this unity . . . so that the Love with which you loved me may be in them and I in them.
>
> John XVII, 22 and XIV, 9

The first three stages are of an active kind, where the being takes itself by the hand: 'Come close to God and He will come close to you' (James: IV, 8). The other two are phases of abandonment, of offering: the being lets himself be taken. Coming close to the expressive power of the Word means allowing oneself to be captured and absorbed, like a body that goes too near the centre of gravity of the sun.

The being becomes free only when it learns to eliminate in itself what previously turned him away from the Father-Principle in which 'it is, moves and lives'. The key to the achievement of this process of liberation is Love, and the *yoga* of Love is the *sādhanā*-raft to take us across the ocean of slavery. Initiation into the mystery of the Kingdom of Love brings the disciple among those who *are*.

Baptism-Purification

As far as the purification (*yama* and *niyama*, the first two *aṅgas* of *Rāja-yoga*) is concerned there are many techniques; we shall take a brief look at only three of these, which are really different phases of a single process.

The first favours the withdrawing of the consciential Centre in such a way as to create a 'distance' with the entire reactive psychic world.

The second works by using a *mantra* (sound of syllables) which have the power of ultrasounds, so as to dissolve subconscious contents.

The third promotes the stabilization of the point at the centre of consciousness, allowing further progress to be made.

With these three movements the embodied reflection of consciousness shifts from the peripheral area of its psycho-physical compound to the centre; the discording sounds of inferior nature are weakened and slowly annulled; reactive individuality reduces itself to silence, making itself available to the fire of transfiguration.

Purification does not involve only strengthening moral qualities (moral in the ordinary sense of the term), but implies *transforming* the vibratory state of the entire individual. Psycho-physical individuality is a vibratory complex which may resound harmony or discord; an emotional or energetic current of hate, for example, can influence the whole surrounding area; those who have a well-trained *eye* are able to capture disturbances produced within the environment.

During the process of purification if daring, discrimination and detachment (*vairāgya*) and so on are lacking, individuality cannot be brought to the necessary level, and transfiguration, with subsequent crucifixion or *death* of the Adamic complex, will not take place. 'New wine cannot be put in old vats.' In this first stage the *mantra* intervenes to solve the problem of subconscious fossilization.

Man is bound by the gravitational strength of his own crystallized, petrified, solidified world (*vāsanā*). A psychic content is an energetical coagulation permeated by a particular tendency (*saṁskāra*); it is a piece of ice which must be brought back to the liquid state; mass must be transformed into energy.

A dualism between the deliberating consciousness of the moment and the subconscious content frequently occurs. The consciousness decides to operate in a certain manner, but the subconsciousness opposes this decision, and often wins out.

> In fact, if we have become one plant with Him, due to a death like His, then we shall surely be one with Him due to a resurrection like His. We know that our old self has been crucified with Him so that the sinful body might be destroyed and we might be no longer enslaved by sin, because He who is dead is free from sin.
>
> Paul to the Romans: VI, 5ff

> I do not understand my own actions, for I do not act as I wish, but I do the very things I hate . . . I can will what is right but I cannot do it . . . So I find it to be a law that when I want to do right, evil lies close at hand.
>
> *Ibid.*: VII, 15ff

> . . . But I say, walk by the Spirit, and do not gratify the desires of the flesh. For the desires of the flesh are against the Spirit and the desires of the Spirit against the flesh: for these are opposite to each other, to prevent you from doing what you would.
>
> Paul to the Galatians: V, 16ff

The struggle must be undertaken by the individual with intelligence, with adequate training, and with appropriate stimulation. Even though all action is supported by the grace of divine Love, it is always the individual who must act at various levels. If he does not do so he may fall into sterile passivity and inertia. It would be too easy for the ego to let the divine Power lift it up out of the hell into which it has allowed itself to fall. During the preliminary phases one must watch out for the sophisms that the ego may advance.

With the intelligent action of the individual and the Love of the all-pervading Principle victory cannot fail to be achieved: 'Be willing, I have overcome the world.'

Transfiguration

At the advanced, but gradual, process of solution of the subconscious vibratory aggregate (the crystallized evil-egoism which opposes Good-Love), one is already within the transfiguration phase.

During the process the consciousness, freed from the Adamic vibratory disharmony and gravity, is ready to sound another *mantra* which represents a *harmonic* of the note of universal Love. This must be vibrated in the right place in order to open up in us that 'window' which leads us to the desired plane. Love can begin to take root in the heart when egoism has loosened its grip. One cannot love while remaining an egoist; one cannot know while remaining ignorant.

The work of transfiguration implies profound withdrawal into oneself, solitude and psychic silence. It is a question of being able to tune the 'ear' to the subtle, supraphysical musicality of the inner Christ. This involves invocation, evocation, precipitation and stabilization of the universal Sound within one's own heart. Christ played the note of Love upon three existential levels: the causal, the manifested universal (subtle) and the gross-physical by means of the vibrated *word*. The two notes of the physical and the subtle (gross and hyper-physical manifestation) are the *harmonics* of the fundamental Note which is the immortal Word upon its own plane (*śabdabrahman*).

Gradually the man-compound is transformed, and the consciousness *understands* that Reality itself, in its essential and noetical dimension, cannot be conceived in terms of empirical, subject-object knowledge. Rational discriminations, like conceptual definitions, vanish because they lose their motive and aim; thought is faced with its own failure and has to recognize, beyond its own existence and workings, that innocent and joyful Beauty of infinite Love, together with Knowledge as its inherent aspect. Thought, the anxiety to learn through the senses, anguish due to the impotence which mortifies and petrifies, all fall silent because in the end they are overpowered by that *pax profunda* where all thinking and speaking become inane absurdities.

The Soul finds itself suspended between the

extreme limit of the One-Father who is set over everything, and the negativeness of the Adamic nature which generates chaos and dark rebellion. But the Love-knowledge which by now penetrates into and shines within the centre of the re-oriented Soul makes clear that not without, but deeper and deeper within itself, it may find the source of its sublimeness and of its transcendence. This implies that the two *cakras* or centres, *anāhata* and *ājñā,* are harmonizing and becoming integrated; mind and soul are merging, Love is pervaded by Knowledge and Knowledge by Love; at the same time the centre at the top of the head, the *sahasrāra,* synthesis of all the *cakras* and seat of the transcendent Spirit, begins to be activated.

Upon the Mount of the divine Transfiguration, *avidyā* (metaphysical ignorance) blurs until it is dispersed inexorably by the joyful rays of Love-knowledge, the Power that has within itself the Fullness as peace and bliss commensurate with the Divinity. In this state of consciousness, the Soul no longer strives towards the satisfaction of exterior and profane appetites, but longs to achieve immobile Identity with the Spirit. When it can quench the outward motion of the powers, it flows back into the integral primordial state, tasting the joy and the happiness of Harmony, of Love and of Knowledge.

. . . As Dionysius (in the second chapter of the *De*

> *Div. Nom.*) says, Hierotheo is perfect in divine things not only because he knows them but because he experiences them within himself.
>
> St. Thomas

Crucifixion-Death

This imponderable motion of re-entry, of penetration into the bottomless depth of Life, leads individuality to *death*, to the crucifixion of the *natured*, of the multiple, of becoming, of the dispersive.

Father Philipon says in his work *The Spiritual Doctrine*, quoted by P. Marin in *Theology of Christian Perfection*:

> While the gift of science moves in an ascensional direction to raise the soul of creatures up to God, while the gift of the intellect penetrates, with a simple glance of love, all the mysteries of God within and without, the gift of knowledge never leaves, as it were, the very heart of the Trinity. All is seen from this indivisible Centre . . . It is the glance of the 'Word which inspires Love' . . . Introduced . . . into the infinite abyss of the Divine Persons, almost within their intimate life, the deified soul, under the impulse of the Spirit of Love, contemplates all from this height . . .

Christ is no longer seen in a static (physical) form but in a dynamic (subtle), operative one; no longer outside one's own consciousness but within it; no longer as something to adore, but to *reveal*. While this process takes place and produces catharsis, the *mantra*-sound represents the sound-note of Christ; it is transfigured into the subtle Note of Love.

The being perceives that it is just vibration of Love, it is neither an individuality nor a *particular* entity; it is only vibrant Love because Christ is cohesive Sound, harmonic tonal accord revealing omni-comprehension, the Centre of the universe, the fundamental note that resounds in space (*ākāśa*), the rejoicing *mantra*. What is conceived as Christ becomes authentic divine Word which harmonizes, with its rhythm, the spheres of life. All entities are seen as a close network of luminous geometrical points creating perfect symmetry; Love creates eurythmy, renders space assonant and the geometrical points commensurate.

Before reaching this level, however, one must pay great attention to what one perceives: sounds, forms and non-formal colours. What one sees is always a 'second' that has no absolute reality. It is not a question of seeing or of stepping beside oneself, but of *being*; it is not a question of observing the form-effigy-image of Christ, but of *being* a vibration of Christ love.

Ascension and Union

Love is at last freed from instinct, from emotion-sentiment and from psychic conceptualism; by returning to being pure motion of the Spirit, unconditioned by the influence of the individualized, it discovers its *freedom*, because Love, insofar as it is pure spiritual essence, is true freedom, while desire is a prison.

Love makes one free because it *is* freedom; passionate desire produces slaves because it is itself slavery. Moreover, to detach the energy of Love from all superimpositions of concepts, of sentiment and of instinct means that Love no longer *adheres* to objective aspects of any kind or degree. Love for the Principle is not only for mine, yours, his or hers, nor is it conditioned by any particular creed; if this were to occur, it would mean adhering to the single, the selective, the exclusive, which are all products of desire.

Love is like the wind that goes where it wishes; it is like the sun which shines on the just and the unjust, on saints and sinners.

> Love your enemies and pray for those who persecute you, so that you may be sons of your Father who is in Heaven; for He makes the sun rise on the evil and the good, and sends rain on the just and on the unjust.
>
> Matthew: V, 44–45

Love, freed from profane and spiritual passion, glows of a light uncontaminated by manasic dialectics.

In *savikalpa samādhi*, being goes beyond names and forms and *ascends* absorbed by the potent original and causal vibration of Love. A grafting takes place, like when a river joins a larger stream realizing itself as unity. This *samādhi* reveals Love as it appears upon the various planes of existence. Although it is unity, it understands the apparent expressive multiplicity of the fundamental Note.

That *mantra*-sound used during the previous phases is no longer *heard* either at gross level or at subtle level because now one *is* the essence itself of universal Sound; or because it has been dissolved in the Word which penetrates and vitalizes all; the Soul itself has dissolved into pure Spirit:

> But he who is united to the Lord becomes one Spirit with Him.
>
> Paul to the Corinthians: VI, 17

An *avatāra* is the incarnation of a divine Principle which reveals itself by means of a temporary form upon a specific existential level.

Christ did not come to comfort the psyche of the fallen Adam, he did not come to back the lazy, nor to place upon the altar the emotional sufferings of men, but to bring the wandering son back to the Father through Initiation into the Mysteries of Christ's Love; an Initiation which involves *purification, transfiguration, crucifixion, ascension* and *union.*

These phases of initiation can be carried out by means of the *yoga* of Love (*Prema-yoga*), the *yoga* of resolving Fire.

[1] On the question of the 'fall' see the chapter 'The Fall of the Soul' in *The Pathway of Non-duality* by Raphael, op. cit.

7

Rāja-yoga

The *Yoga-sūtra* or *Rāja-yoga*[1] (royal *Yoga*), codified by Patañjali, aims at the suspension-solution of the modifications of the mind (*citta-vṛtti-nirodha*). When this has been accomplished and stabilized, then the Seer (pure Consciousness, *puruṣa* or the real entity) is founded upon his own nature, which implies that he is no longer *necessitated* by the movement of the *prakṛti*-substance-nature.

What are the 'mental modifications'? They are the endless requests, conceptions, projections, extrovert movements of the mind. These movements, in turn, are caused by what we call *desire*. Desire urges the mental substance to work towards satisfaction and gratification. Desire is a breach of equilibrium, an upsetting of a pre-established order.

But why do we desire? Because we do not know

our true nature, because we have *forgotten* what we really are and therefore we are obliged to yearn for some object. Once we have veiled our true being which *is* and does not become, it is obvious that we must content ourselves with surrogates, with things that, however gratifying they may appear to be, can never take the place of the nature of being, which is Fullness or Bliss without an object.

But what are we really? For *Yoga-sūtra* (and for the entire Vedic-mysteric initiatory Tradition) we are immortal, self-shining Beings, we are *puruṣas* (universal Lords), we are eternal Souls which 'are what they are', we are self-existing *ātman* which depends upon nothing.

But how can we recognize our immortal nature? Not, certainly, through simple mental conceptualization or by producing further illusory *vṛttis,* but by carrying out *Yoga-sūtra,* that is by suspending our 'mental modifications'. In this way we arrive at the Essence of what we really are. By stopping becoming in ourselves, Being is revealed. For example, how can the simplest of all elements, hydrogen, be found? By breaking up a chemical compound until we get to the essence of what chemical compounds are. At human level there are geniuses who have intuition, who theorize and enounce certain truths (and these are true pioneers); there are others who wish to experience 'empirically' those enounced truths.

Yoga, in its true sense, is the empirical, pragmatic, operative aspect used to reveal the fundamental truth which *yoga* itself enounces. Seen in this sense, *yoga* is 'experimental vision'; it is theory and practice, and these two aspects must be integrated if one wants to achieve the proper results. *Yoga* can tell you: you are the immortal and supreme Lord of yourself and I give you the practical and operative means for demonstrating and revealing this truth.

Many are agnostics 'on principle', they are absolutists in their denial; the reasons for this kind of behaviour are very varied, and of many different types. While *yoga* holds that the 'mental modifications' (*vṛttis*) can be curbed, suspended and even transcended, it also offers the practical means by which to achieve this proposition; if some cannot reach this goal for certain reasons, others who possess the necessary qualifications will be able to do so.

If, therefore, desire is a lack, a want of something, a necessity, our consciousness identifies with something relative and dependent, with a factor that is not *causa sui*, which is not founded upon itself. It is obvious that all that is not based upon itself must find completeness and gratification in other things. This identification of the *puruṣa*'s consciential reflection with fleeting and unstable things in *yoga* terms is called *avidyā*.

Avidyā means taking the non-eternal, the contingent and the relative for the absolute; that means, taking the non-real for the real (II, 5). Thus, *avidyā* – being the cause of identification with the non-real – is the root of all *kleṣas* (afflictions) of which Patañjali speaks in chapter II, *sūtra* 3ff. All that is visible, objective, manifested, produced by *prakṛti* represents the contingent, the relative, non-being, the world of names and forms that comes and goes, that appears and disappears, which is subject to duality-polarity, while *he* who sees is a Seer or an immortal *puruṣa*. What must be avoided is the *identification* of the Seer with the visible (II, 17).

From these *sūtras* one can grasp the fact that *avidyā*, being the cause of obscurity and of oblivion of self, obliges us to create a false ego-self (*asmitā*, or the sense of individuality, or of 'I am this separate self') which, not being based upon itself, creates attachment-attraction towards something and also dislike-repulsion; the ego, pushed thus from one pole (pleasure) to another (pain) is obliged to seek experience (*abhiniveśa*) in the vain belief of finding gratification and happiness. But pleasure-pain, a quality typical of the world of names and forms, is a two-sided coin; indeed, according to Patañjali, pleasure itself, owing to the simple fact of being a surrogate and fleeting factor, carries with it.

Avidyā obliges us to believe the immortal to be mortal, the absolute relative, the non-real real. Thus the entity, under the effect of *avidyā*, thinks that it is mortal, dependent, needy, dual, and so on, with all the consequences that such a view-point or belief may bring about. The visible (therefore the gross physical body also and the other subtler bodies possessed by the entity) is only a means through which the *puruṣa*-being can reveal itself. The appropriation (even with violence) of the visible – of every degree and order whatsoever – is the outcome of believing it to be absolutely necessary, a source of absolute happiness and gratification, when it is really alienation, conflict and pain. Through this deformed vision truth itself is subverted: the visible becomes absolute-real and the Seer a subjected effect, at times even ignored and negated.

The false and illusory 'I' becomes real and true; the Self, the *puruṣa,* the *ātman,* the 'true Man', the Seer becomes unreal. But the visible-*prakṛti* is but an instrument in the hands of the Seer (II, 21); indeed, this visible dimension disappears altogether (it is integrated and transcended) by the liberated one, while it still exists for those who must yet free themselves (II, 22). In fact, the solution of the Seer's assimilation to the visible, produced by *avidyā,* is the sure remedy and represents his liberation (II, 25).

To achieve the Seer's detachment from the visible, *Yoga-sūtra* – contrary to what is usually believed – indicates various practical ways: surrender to *Īśvara, viveka-vairāgya* and the eight *aṅgas* (means).

SURRENDER TO ĪŚVARA

Surrender to *Īśvara* concerns *Bhakti* (love-devotion), and therefore the *Yoga-sūtra* also includes *Bhakti*. Patañjali speaks of surrender to *Īśvara* in I–23, II–32 and II–45.

What is meant by *Īśvara*? *Īśvara* is the supreme *Puruṣa* untouched by the afflictions of life, by actions or by their results (I, 24). Patañjali's *Yoga*, being a *darśana*, is based upon the *Vedas* and upon the *Upaniṣads* and therefore it is not outside the context of the pure Vedic-Upanishadic Tradition; its tenets are largely those of the *Sāṁkhya*, which is another *darśana*. Thus, within the traditional context, *Īśvara* is the supreme *Puruṣa*, and the various existent *puruṣas* are but its 'consciential moments'. Surrender to *Īśvara* implies considering oneself no longer as a separate entity, but as an integral part of the *Īśvara*'s unity. From this comes *yoga* which means 'to join', to unite, to re-integrate, to merge the particular with the universal, the individual 'this' with the universal *That*.

Rāja-yoga represents, therefore, the means by which the separated individual becomes once more universal Unity, because the nature of the entity is universal, it is divine, suprasensible, consciential unity. The fulfilment-perfection of the *samādhi*, which after all is nothing but the 'suspension of the mental modifications' in its entirety, can therefore be achieved through the surrender to *Īśvara* (*Īśvara praṇidhānāt*, II, 45). How? The *citta-vṛttis* are caused by *avidyā* and the *vṛttis* produce attachment to the visible. Now, if that potent energy-love-aspiration-*eros* directed towards the external visible world is turned towards the transcendent *Īśvara,* or our divine counterpart, a total conversion, a detachment from what is visible and conflictual, takes place naturally. In other words, if desire for *things* is transformed into Love, this 'makes wings grow' upon the 'fallen' *puruṣa* so that it can fly towards the divine essence. It represents the Platonic *Eros* which expresses itself as 'thirst for the Divine' and not as thirst for the things that are *not.*

The thirst of the *puruṣa* who believes itself an individual (*asmitā,* 'I am this', II, 6) can be quenched only by using the Water that quenches thirst forever; it is the Vedic *soma. Īśvara praṇidhāna* produces *para-vairāgya,* supreme detachment; it breaks the chains of contingent desire, it dissolves conflictual *citta-vṛttis* and the loving *puruṣa* fuses with the Beloved *Parapuruṣa* (supreme *Puruṣa*).

VIVEKA-VAIRĀGYA

We also mentioned *viveka-vairāgya* as a *yoga* means of realization. 'For whoever has developed discrimination-discernment (*viveka*) everything turns out to be suffering . . .' (II, 15). If intuitive discernment makes us recognize that the relative and dual visible is not the ultimate Reality, then this visible can never give constant Bliss nor stable knowledge and therefore it follows that consciential detachment (*vairāgya*) – and not just formal detachment – from the conflicting visible cannot but lead one to be what one is. Besides, *viveka* and *vairāgya* are particularly the two techniques of the *Vedānta darśana*.

> Non-attachment (*vairāgya*) is that conscious self-mastery of he who has ceased to thirst for visible and audible objects. That supreme [detachment] is represented by total liberation from the *guṇas* as a result of the *Puruṣa* becoming conscious of itself.
>
> *Yoga-sūtra*: I, 15–16[2]

Non-attachment or detachment, in order not to be a mere forced withdrawing upon oneself, must have as a base intuitive discernment, discrimination between what is eternal, immortal, absolute and what is not; between what is Being insofar as it *is* and does not become and what is pure appearance, surrogate and accidental. Thus, *viveka* is the fruit of knowledge (*jñāna*), or gnosis, which is capable of revealing the ultimate and real nature of things. And when cognitive discernment indicates that phenomenon-appearance, although it participates in the reality of Being, is not Reality as such, then the *puruṣa*-knower can no longer identify with appearance taking it for reality, and by not attaching itself to it any longer defeats *avidyā* and attains *kaivalya*, supreme Liberation.

Kaivalya follows upon re-absortion of the *guṇas* because they lose all meaning for the *puruṣá* or [one achieves *kaivalya*] when consciousness is founded upon its own essence.

Yoga-sūtra: IV, 34[3]

The Eight Means or Aṅgas

Rāja-yoga places emphasis on the mind rather than on the body or the emotions. It seeks to control *citta*, the mental substance, with all its products: the *vṛttis* or thought-waves which, if not controlled, lead the *jīva* (incarnated soul) into the flow of *saṁsāra*.

The position of *Rāja-yoga* is clear: the *prāṇa* complex of the body and of the sensory emotions depend upon the mind (*manas*); if this were not to work then the gross physical sphere and that of the more subtle senses would simply be automatons. Perception takes place upon the mental plane; feelings are perceived by the mind, and the body itself can be dominated and directed by a mind that has understood its own movement. As in the case of physical science where, by controlling atomic energy processes in an automatic way, one controls the molecular energy and that of the external tissues, by controlling *citta* and the *vṛttis* the whole psychic-sensorial process is subdued and directed.

Within an individual, the mental sphere is the highest, and the one that synthesizes all the factors from a *prāṇa*-energetic and mass point of view. It is therefore extremely important, and *Rāja-yoga* or Patañjali's *Yoga-sūtra* dedicates all its attention to it, even if it makes use of positions (*āsanas*) and of *prāṇāyāma*, the pillars of *Haṭha-yoga*. *Rāja* is the royal *yoga*: it synthesizes in a central point of the mind the entire individuality of the *jīva* on the way.

Another merit that must be attributed to *Rāja-yoga* is that it begins its *sādhanā* with purification of the emotions and of the mind. Without a preliminary cleansing of undesirable psychic contents, this type of *yoga* may prove to be very dangerous, not only at the *manas* level but also at the physical level. According to the classical *darśana* the purifying act is divided into two phases which correspond with the five *yamas* and the five *niyamas*, the first two of the eight *aṅgas* (means) of *Rāja-yoga*.

The *yamas* are rules regarding moral conduct; one must seek the truth, abstain from doing evil, from stealing, from coercing, and so on. They imply domination of the *rajas*' tendencies (*rajo-guṇa*) which urge one towards acquisitions, give rise to passion, to egoism. The main aim of these rules is to quench the thirst of the possessive extroversion and therefore of the *rajo-guṇa*, to empty one's mind of excessively conditioning contents which are a strong obstacle to a specific activity aimed at psycho-physical orientation.

The *niyamas* too belong to the sphere of 'discipline'

and allow the mental energies to model themselves according to the rhythm of *sattva*.

Rāja-yoga may be undertaken without fear if the preliminary phase of discipline has been carried out so that it has become habitual. True withdrawal or abstraction of the consciousness from the senses (*pratyāhāra*) will take place easily if the mind has been purified. Thus, in turn, concentration (*dhāraṇā*), meditation (*dhyāna*) and *samādhi* can be achieved if an actual withdrawal of the consciousness from the objects of sense has been accomplished.

Rāja-yoga does not aim solely at quelling turbulent thought modifications, nor does it aim at inculcating certain rules of moral conduct; it goes much further because its true purpose is that of slowing down the movement of the three *guṇas* (which produce objectifying and restless activity on the part of the *puruṣa-jīva*) until they are totally absorbed into *prakṛti* (primigenial substance), thus leaving the *puruṣa-jīva* utterly free. This condition is called *kaivalya*. In the *kaivalya* state, the *puruṣa* founds in its own nature, which is pure awareness, devoid of translational motion around *prakṛti*'s object-events. It is necessary, in any case, to consider *Rāja-yoga* as the pathway of the ardent will, that of the enflamed disciple who 'wants to be'. The will to reach the Divine is such that the willful disciple is capable of subduing his inferior instances and brings to the altar of the Divinity a changed and transfigured being. There are no obstacles to the will that seeks the Supreme.

But what places obstacles against union? What impedes spiritual advancement and consummation? *Rāja-yoga*'s answer is: undisciplined human-animal nature which renders the neophyte a slave to the world of incompleteness. It is the restless and inconstant mind which creates distance and separation. Thus, an individual who wishes to reach perfection must direct his efforts towards dominating his own inferior nature, change and sublimate all his energies so as to project them, pure and cleansed, towards the object of his will. If in *Bhakti* it is the deep devotion, dedication and surrender to the Divinity which urges the disciple towards sublime Union, here it is the *will* to be *kaivalya* which causes a dynamic action of constant elevation until true possession is achieved.

Rāja-yoga is for those who wish to dominate, mould and direct their own nature; it is also a conscious method of redemption because through it all the lower vibrations of the being are sublimated. The active will of *Rāji-yogi* is the upper octave of the *bhakta*'s sentiment-desire.

'By forcefully training the will,' says Radhakrishnan, 'we can achieve the suppression of thoughts that are so keenly felt within our mind, and of mean desires. By means of an active commitment which never stops, the *yogi* is called upon to assume control.'

By means of the *Rāja-yoga* certain powers (*siddhis*)

may develop, but the true *yogi* who is seeking liberation from incompleteness does not care about these, nor is he distracted by them; his is a 'flight' towards *kaivalya*.

Will emerges and manifests itself upon the mental plane just as sentiment-devotion is to be found upon the emotional level. The willful seeker places himself upon the plane of the mind and from there begins his great alchemical-psychic process of transformation.

Rāja-yoga has a positive attitude towards the Divine compared to the receptive attitude of *Bhakti*. In *Rāja-yoga* it is the individual who takes himself by the hand and rises up to the Divine; therefore a psychological knowledge of oneself, an understanding of the mental processes, a knowledge of the subconscious sphere are required, so that the obstacles may be removed and overcome with intelligence, and union achieved.

Rāja means royal, *yoga* union; therefore *Rāja* is that regal *yoga* used to realize union; it synthesizes other types of *yoga* too. Its fundamental notes are meditation (*dhyāna*) and contemplation (*samādhi*), so that it is also called *Dhyāna-yoga* or *Samādhi-yoga*.

Rāja-yoga is a compendium of philosophy, psychology and realizing mysticism. The *Yoga darśana* ('point of view' in reference to the *Vedas*), as we have seen, indicates eight means (*aṅgas*) or stages which lead to final *kaivalya* consisting in liberation of the *Puruṣa*-Spirit from *prakṛti*'s modifications (*prakṛti* or primigenial substance; the 'primordial waters').

Let us summarize the eight means: *yama* (self-restraint), *niyama* (observance), *āsana* (positions), *prāṇāyāma* (control of *prāṇa* breathing), *pratyāhāra* (abstraction), *dhāraṇā* (concentration), *dhyāna* (meditation), *samādhi* (contemplation-ecstasy).

We shall now take a closer look at *dhāraṇā*, *dhyāna* and *samādhi*.

Dhāraṇā

Dhāraṇā consists in fixing the mind upon a *pratyaya* (seed-content of concentration), excluding from the mental field all other possible *pratyayas* that could enter it. This, therefore, is the mind's first act of concentration. It is easy to understand this *aṅga*'s importance if we recognize the fact that the mind always tends to be 'dispersive', to jump around, to be pressed by the necessity of psychic becoming, authentic *saṁsāra*. The being must learn how to retire to the centre of its psycho-physical system and from there begin to put right its 'inner damage'. A mind that is not concentrated cannot be creative; a restless and dispersive mind is typical of one who is subject to the world of *māyā-avidyā*.

Mental restlessness is brought about by the continuous stimuli of the subconsciousness and of an over-sensitive and impressionable emotional body.

To eliminate this cause of restlessness one must practise the first five *aṅgas* which have this preliminary function.

The infra-psychic world is *chaos*; one must create a *cosmos* by taking the Soul gradually back to its pre-Adamic condition. The first act is to place oneself at the centre of one's own psycho-physical system, and *dhāraṇā* represents this position of consciousness. Concentration is the outcome of attention; where there is attention there is concentration, whereby all the 'powers' are fixed upon the relevant *pratyaya*.

Dhyāna

Dhyāna is prolonged concentration and is the basis of all possible creativity; it is the tool by which the senses are dominated. *Dhyāna* opens the door to *samādhi*; *dhyāna* is the royal medium which God has given to man so that he can reach Him. It is the bow by which the disciple-archer hits the Target. *Dhyāna* is the highest psychic faculty after intelligence: intelligence cannot reveal itself in a mind that is not harmonized. With *dhyāna* the psychic powers are co-ordinated, integrated, directed in a conscious and deliberate way on the basis of a pre-established motive. *Dhyāna* is the instrument which can lead to conflict, to error and to pain, or to the bliss of *samādhi*.

Dhyāna consists in a *continuous*, uninterrupted

flow (and here lies the difference between it and *dhāraṇā*) of thought energy towards the *pratyaya* that has been chosen. Our psychic powers, both conscious and unconscious, can be solved only by means of a stable mind, capable and ready to melt or to coagulate them. All sentimental movement, even when it leads to happiness, is but passing and fleeting. If one does not build on the solid foundations of *dhyāna* which is of the mental order, one may become an intermittent and emotional mystic, because emotion without mental direction is unstable, incomplete, excessively individual (it follows the law of attraction-repulsion) and is the cause of grave psychic disturbances, besides being a factor of mere opinion.

Dhyāna may be directed towards a concrete *pratyaya* or towards an abstract one, of a formal order or not, and so it covers a wide range of activity. Thus, meditation can be based upon a *yantra* (a simple or complex geometrical symbol or figure), upon a sound or *mantra,* upon a colour (light), and so on. All these seeds – depending upon the sensitivity of the disciple – bring about the opportune transformations of the consciousness. The symbol is cathartic; it favours transmutation.

Through constant and intelligent exercise one can meditate for hours without the slightest mental distraction, although one may also receive stimuli or disturbances from outside.

A mind under control, at peace and always available is watchful, and according to Buddhist tradition watchfulness can lead to *Nirvāṇa*.

'In the beginning was the Word, and the Word was with God, and the Word was God.' The Verbum is the Word of power and the Word is *sound*. Sound is vibration which produces specific effects. We know from science that sound is both creator and destroyer. The sound impressed its notes upon the 'primordial waters'. The creating principle of the Word is also possessed by the human being 'made to the likeness of the Creator'.

By means of meditation using sound (*mantra*), forms (*yantra*), and so on, the individual produces certain specific results upon the 'waters' or psycho-physical substance. Sound, for example, is a vibrated Idea; by vibrating in deep meditation some *bīja*-seeds or sounds, *space*, which is life, responds. *Mantras* are *powers* resounding in infinite space; they may be picked up and transmitted, like the Vedic *Ṛṣis* have done.

God thought (Word) and the worlds emerged from the abyss of darkness. Sound at certain levels becomes Light (hence the *dhyāna* upon colour) which triumphs over darkness.

With *dhāraṇā* one fixes the creative mind-instrument; with *dhyāna* one pronounces the Idea-seed-word; with *samādhi* one realizes the subject-object unity or the incarnation of the Word.

Prayer is the expression of emotion, meditation

is the mind's act of power, while *samādhi* is the work of *buddhi* (another of the Soul's bodies of manifestation).

We can summarize the meditation process by giving some correlations:

Mantra	Sound	Spirit-*ātman*
Colour	Quality-Light	Soul-*jīvātman*
Yantra	Form or plane	Body-*sthūlaśarīra*

These three notes can be resounded within particular *cakras* or vital centres, in order to create certain pre-established effects; they may also be combined with *prāṇāyāma, prāṇa* breathing and *mudrās* (gestures).

If one keeps in mind that the *jīvātman* (Soul) – the reflection of *ātman* – lives in the heart's most secret and inner folds and that many sensory-manasic superimpositions hide it, one can appreciate the enormous importance of these meditation techniques.

The reconquest of pre-Adamic nature is a task of initiation and not of simple *manas* (mental) speculation or of voicing the name of the Father.

Samādhi

Incisive and steadfast meditation upon a *pratyaya* leads to *samādhi*. These three aspects – *dhāraṇā, dhyāna* and *samādhi* – are but three stages of the same process; in fact, the three taken together are called *saṁyama*. To practise *saṁyama* upon a *pratyaya* means entering gradually into *samādhi*.

> Grasping the potent weapon (*Om*) of the *Upaniṣads* like a bow, knock in it the arrow sharpened by contemplation and cover it with intention in conformity with its Essence.
>
> *Om* is the bow, the *ātman* the arrow, *Brahma* the target; wi thout distraction, this has to be hit rendering oneself similar to an arrow (which flies to join the target).
>
> *Muṇḍaka-up.*: II, ii, 3–4

Samādhi is characterized by various phases; in its last stage it represents penetration of the *essence* of the *pratyaya*, the realization of its ultimate identity, beyond the realm of subject-object.

By translating *samādhi* with the word 'contemplation' one risks improverishing the original Sanskrit term, seeing that in general in the West contemplation means simple visualization of a datum.

Samādhi, first of all, is related neither to emotions nor to the imagination nor to any individualized psychic power. On the *dhyāna* plane one is within the sphere of dualism and of the objective; with *samādhi* one goes beyond empirical and objective dualism and enters into *subtle* dimensions. A state of happiness, for example, can be evoked with the emotions; it can be imagined and guessed at, but these things concern the psychic sphere within which the subject-object works. Experiencing happiness with one's whole consciousness is quite different. It is one thing to imagine or 'to have in front of oneself', and another thing *to be.*

Samādhi, in its true sense, is direct experience of truth without the intervention of *manas* (the empirical rational mind) and, as there are different degrees of the sole Reality-truth, there are also different degrees of *samādhi. Rāja-yoga* lists some of them.

First of all we have two categories of *samādhi*: with seed or *bīja* and without seed, that is *saṁprajñāta samādhi* and *asaṁprajñāta samādhi,* or *sabīja saīādhi* and *nirbīja samādhi.*

Saṁprajñāta samādhi can be thus divided:

1. *savitarka* and *nirvitarka*
2. *savicāra* and *nirvicāra*
3. *sānanda* and *nirānanda*
4. *sasmitā* and *nirasmitā*

In order to understand these terms it is important to consider that every *datum* has two aspects: *rūpa* (objective form) and *svarūpa* (the very essence of the datum).

In the case of the *manas*-mind as found in the *dhyāna* state, the *rūpa* is the *pratyaya* of meditation, the formal object; the *svarūpa,* on the other hand, coincides with the subjective nature of the mind itself, separated from its ideal content. Thus, the *savitarka* and *nirvitarka* degree, for example, respond to the objective and non-objective functional condition; these states indicate simply the function of *citta* (total psychic content) rather than the level upon which it operates. That is, they concern more the function than the substantial structure of the level of manifestation.

In order to better grasp these functions we can relate them to the planes or to the vehicles which the Soul uses to express itself upon the various levels of existence.

Savitarka is the function of mind-*manas* upon the subtle plane of *manas,* separated from objective material data; *savicāra* is the function of the *buddhimayakośa* or *vijñānamayakośa* (vehicle made of intellect), separated from *manas* conditioning; *sānanda* is the function of *ānandamayakośa* (sheath, vehicle or body for the expression of bliss) abstracted from the *buddhi* support; *sasmitā* is the function of the *jīva* in its essential selfness, separated from all bodies of manifestation. Only that consciousness which dwells in itself, lives for itself and with itself exists on the plane of *jīva* or *ātmā,* on the plane of the purified Soul. In the *sānanda samādhi* there subsist: the entity (*svarūpa*) and the object-*bīja* (*rūpa*) represented by *avidyā* (primordial ignorance); in the *sasmitā samādhi* the entity is abstracted from its *rūpa* and is ready to re-integrate itself with the pure Spirit, with the *Brahman-ātman* or, in the specific case of *Rāja-yoga,* with the sovereign *Puruṣa.* These last two *samādhis* may be expressed conceptually as 'I am this' and as 'I am', while in *asaṁprajñāta samādhi* or *nirbīja samādhi* the 'I am' is dissolved into *That* or *Turīya* for *Advaita Vedānta* and into *Puruṣa* isolated from *ahaṁkāra* (sense of ego) and from the modifications of *prakṛti* for *Rāja-yoga.*[4]

[1] Cp. Patañjali, *The Regal Way of Realization – Yogadarśana.* Translation from the Sanskrit and commentary by Raphael. Edizioni Āśram Vidyā, Roma 1992.

[2] Patañjali, *Op. cit.*

[3] *Ibid.*

[4] For further details concerning the various types of *samādhi,* cp. *Self and Non-self* (*The Dṛg-dṛśya-viveka*) translation from the Sanskrit and commentary by Raphael, Edizioni Āśram Vidyā, Rome 1983, (English Translation by Kegan Paul International Ltd, London 1990).

8

Jñāna-yoga

Jñāna-yoga, or the *yoga* of knowledge, aims above all at 'knowing' the Divinity.

If God is the ultimate Truth, the Reality amid all possible truths, then all that is not God is ignorance, blindness and illusion. Thus, the purpose of *jñāna* is to remove ignorance and darkness and grasp the Truth and the Light. To travel this path the disciple needs a developed, sensitive mind, open to the problems of Being and Non-Being.

The great aspiration of the *jñāni* is the 'quest' for the absolute Truth, not partial truths, because this is examined and discovered by the selective-analytical mind (*manas*).

Only when Truth has been discovered can the disciple immerse himself into what he always desired, by means of an act of 'self-identification and incarnation'. The *jñāni* is he who incarnates and manifests Knowledge.

He is faced with three factors to resolve:

the knowing subject
knowledge
the object of knowledge

Slowly these three factors are fused together and become one. The *jñāni* can realize Truth because he himself is Truth. By means of knowledge, the object is assimilated into the knowing subject. This is neither the way of the scientist nor of the theologian nor of the simple intellectual, as might appear at first, but it is the way of the intuitive-contemplative philosopher (Socrates, Plato, Plotinus, Śaṁkara), of the metaphysician; it is the way of the person who operates using that kind of synthetical, plastic, extrasensible thinking that leads to 'immediate Discernment'.

Jñāna research is made of Silences, of Intuitions, of Illuminations, of Visions, of the discovery of the noumenon, of detachment and dispassion. It is not the way of passive devotion towards the Being about which one wishes to know nothing, nor the way made of acts of deliberate will, nor the way of action, but it is the way of 'intuitive discernment'; it is the way that penetrates the ultimate mysteries of Reality, it is the path that works using Ideas and archetypical and synthetical ideal Principles. It is a pathway of solitude, of abstractions; it requires time and prolonged contemplation which is not of a sensible-devotional kind.

It might appear to be the pathway of the West, and yet it is not: the western mind is more analytical, critical, discursive, extrovert. The western person is more inclined towards activism, and is taken up more with the construction of material things, with creating the means by which to gratify the physical aspects of being.

To travel along this kind of road it is necessary instead to withdraw into oneself, to create a centripetal movement; to have a mind capable of grasping in an effortless way the objective manifestation and the inner life, a capacity for deduction, an understanding of the connections between life and form, between spirit and matter, God and nature, cause and effect, an attitude for searching the world of *meanings*, an immense thirst for spiritual Truth, a constant, daily meditative-contemplative attitude. Little by little, as the disciple removes what *is not*, he lives and incarnates what *is*.

> And you will know Truth, and Truth will make you free.
>
> John: VIII, 32

This is the motto of the *jñāni*; he thus concentrates all his resources in order to come into possession of Truth and *to be* Truth.

'The way of Knowledge,' says Aurobindo, 'aims at the realization of the sole supreme Self. It seeks proper discernment, observes and distinguishes between the different elements of our apparent and phenomenal being, and refusing to identify itself with them it arrives at excluding them as components of *prakṛti* or creations of *māyā*, as phenomenal consciousness and thus arrives at the identification with the sole and pure Self, which is unchanging and imperishable and which cannot be defined by any phenomenon or combination of phenomena. From this instant the phenomenal world is excluded from consciousness as it is but an illusion, and final immersion without return is achieved by the Soul in the Supreme.'

Here are some *sūtras* by Svāmi Śivānanda taken from the book *Jñāna-yoga*, and a few passages from *Le chemin de la perfection selon le Yoga Vedānta* by Svāmi Nityabodhānanda, interspersed with some considerations of ours.[1]

> *Jñāna-yoga* is the 'royal way' and is described in all the practical treatises of *Vedānta*. The starting point is a deep spiritual perception of the Vedantic texts with the help of a qualified instructor. Only the *Upaniṣads* can give a precise knowledge of *Brahman*. Listening to them, from first to last, can convince the listener of the extreme importance of all the sacred texts, and show him the identity of the individual soul with the only Soul or *Brahman*. When listening to them all doubts concerning the value of the Vedantic Scriptures, the

recognized traditional source of brahmanic knowledge, vanish.

The second step involves *understanding* what has been *heard*. Reason has a right to examine the Scriptures from many points of view; concerning all that regards the nature of *Brahman*, reasoning permits one to discard all objections. Belief in the absoluteness of the Self, grasped by listening and reflection, is matched with *experience*, by meditating upon this Self. Constant meditation reveals all false superimpositions, all the obstacles that come from traces left by past actions, thus revealing the true nature of the Self.

At the moment when one becomes aware of this *ātman* (Self) the world of appearances and its cause, *māyā*, disappear. The aspirant has thus arrived at his destination, becomes *paramahaṁsa*, a perfect being.

> The heart's knot is loosened, all doubts dissolve and all actions cease to produce their fruits when one sees the Supreme and the Non-Supreme.
>
> *Muṇḍaka-up*.: II, III, 9

The same purpose may be reached by contemplating *Brahman* devoid of all attributes. The sacred texts clearly demonstrate that perfect contemplation of the Absolute is another means of liberation: 'This cause may be understood by reflecting upon its nature on the basis of the Vedantic texts , and also by means of contemplation of the Absolute . . .'

A perfect *Jñāna-yogi*, well-versed and moral, is capable of teaching philosophy and meditation even to two disciples with two different mental dispositions . . . (529).

Listening, *reflection* and *meditation* are the three grades of the state of the *jñāni* disciple. Listening must not be confused with simple physical perception; it requires deep attention from a disciplined, humble and open mind. Reflection is not simply analytical, and so it does not come only from the head but is synthetical-intuitive, it springs from the heart. It is a particular way of *understanding*. Meditation is the unveiling of Reality itself. For a *jñāni* to meditate means *to be*.

> *Jñāna-yoga* is the pathway of Knowledge. *Mokṣa* (Liberation) is obtained through the understanding of *Brahman*. Liberation is obtained by realization of the identity of the individual soul with the supreme Soul. The cause of suffering and of slavery is *avidyā* or Ignorance.
>
> The *yogi* 'realizes' that *Brahman* is the life of his life, the soul of his soul. He feels and knows that God is his very life. He realizes that he is one with the Eternal by means of spiritual intuition and not through simple book-learning, dogmas and theories. The *yogi* plunges into constant and intense meditation within the secret of his heart and finds that marvellous pearl which is *ātman*, the greatest of the world's riches.
>
> *Jñāna* is not cognitive knowledge, or mental understanding, it is not instinctive recognition, nor is it an intellectual feeling. It is the direct realization of one's own unity with the supreme Being. It is *paravidyā*. Intellectual conviction alone can never lead to *brahma-jñāna* (530).

The knowledge that is required is beyond simple

analytical perception of the mind. *Jñāna* is the outcome of the comprehension and of the intuitive discernment produced by intellectual discrimination (*viveka*). It is a sort of direct spiritual perception which may be possessed by whoever already has a certain favourable attitude or particular *qualifications*. In every cultural and scientific field one must have, in order to succeed, a particular mental predisposition, a suitable intellectual-intuitive capacity to grasp the secret of the universal. Truth cannot be revealed by the mind alone, but it reveals itself when the intellectual mechanisms react in the proper way. It is not the finite distinctive mind which can comprehend the infinite *Brahman*, it is instead *Brahman* which reveals itself to the being who is ready. The *jñāni* lives in intuitive contemplation; he questions himself, but does not engage in fine arguments to produce sophisticated answers because these would only produce new superimpositions upon the Real-*Brahman*.

> A pure consciousness, bereft of all movement produced by the mind (*nirvikalpa*) is a very rare state. It is possible to enter this kind of *samādhi* but it is extremely difficult to remain there. Only certain beings such as Śaṁkara, Dattātreya, and so on reached the state of pure consciousness (*nirguṇa*) . . . A *jñāni* does not see the world as you see it. He does not see the objects outside of himself, but within. Through perfect knowledge (*jñāna*) he arrives at pure cosmic knowledge (533).

> *Turīya* is the spiritual state in which the mental dimension cannot act because it is completely absorbed by *Brahman*. It is the 'fourth dimension' where Bliss reigns. This is neither inertia nor oblivion nor annihilation. It is a state of absolute awareness which escapes any kind of description. It is the final purpose, it is *mokṣa* or Liberation . . .
>
> When the water in a pot evaporates, the sun's reflection vanishes. When the ego fuses with *Brahman*, when the mental lake dries up, the reflection of the supreme consciousness is eclipsed and the personality disappears. Only the sole Existence remains . . .
>
> In the mind of the *jñāni* (who has reached the knowledge of *Brahman*) all inferior desires are dissolved and the *sattva* (superior) forms survive. In him neither ire nor evil impulses exist any longer. His will is always balanced. Thanks to his inner completeness he has no more afflictions, therefore he rejoices in perfect equanimity in all places and at all times. Even when his body is subjected to suffering, his mind disregards the inconvenience . . .
>
> The *jñāni* mental sphere should not, strictly speaking, be called by that name at all; it is pure Reality. The mind is what moulds the diversity of objects, now that of the *jñāni* is like copper that an alchemical process has transformed into gold . . . A mind which, although participating in the world of objects, remains detached from it may be considered as being like *Brahman* itself (534).

According to Traditional Vedantic Philosophy there are four states of consciousness:

Microcosm	**Macrocosm**
Vaiśvānara	*Virāṭ*
Taijasa	*Hiraṇyagarbha* or *Sūtrātma*
Prājña	*Īśvara*

Turīya – The Fourth – *Brahman*

It is difficult to understand the state of a *jñāni;* it is so high that all prime elements (*tattva*) fall by themselves. Thus, the sole ocean of ether shines; it is pure Knowledge that transcends all pleasure, all formal beauty: these are creations of *māyā* which distract our vision from the supreme experience. The song of birds too is the work of *māyā* but it prevents us from hearing the melody of the sacred syllable *Om.* The state of *Nirvāṇa* is that of *jñāni* . . .

Persevering effort and indomitable energy can lead us to the knowledge of *Brahman.* The *guru* and the books indicate the way and answer many doubts, but direct and intuitive comprehension must emerge from your own experience. A hungry man must himself eat . . .

He who tries to fix his mind upon *Brahman* performs the highest *Karma-yoga,* the greatest sacrifice, perfect charity. There is no need for him to visit sacred places.

Silent knowledge (*jñāna-mauna*) is the state in which the mind is immersed in *Brahman,* therefore not even the slightest trace of 'ego' exists any longer. As there is no longer any mental activity, there is no experiencer either, and every form of *karma* is burnt by the fire of Knowledge.

The incarnated soul (*jīva*) feels different from all the sheath-vehicles (*kośa*) and immerses itself in the Absolute . . .

Intellectual pleasure is superior to that of the senses; the joy of meditation, in turn, surpasses by far intellectual pleasure, while spiritual Bliss produced by supreme Realization is incommensurable and without limits (535).

The Knowledge (*jñāna-yoga*) of *Brahman* or of the Unconditioned is the supreme remedy to all evils and conflicts of life. Reach that Knowledge by means of discrimination (*viveka*), purity and meditation on *Brahman*.

Knowledge of *Brahman* is a raft or a boat which takes you to the other bank: that of immortality. Use it and you will fear no more (536).

As the mind, during deep sleep, assumes a more subtle form so the mental part of a *jñāni* is of a more subtle form than that of a man who is not evolved . . . The body (of the *jñāni*) is necessary to him only to end his *karma* (*prārabdha*), but he is not in the least disturbed by it because he is absolute *Brahman* and not his body . . . A *jñāni* enters the *nirvikalpa-samādhi* through his thought, a *Haṭha-yogi* enters it by awakening *kuṇḍalinī*; the first mode is more difficult than the second.

The wasp takes possession of a larva, it places it in its hive, it stings it several times and then closes the hive. The larva cannot forget the pain caused it by the wasp and thinks so intensely that it transforms itself into a wasp and thus leaves the hive. Thus the *Jñāna-yoga* aspirant, constantly instructed by the Sacred Scriptures and by meditation, with the mental image of *Brahman*, ends up by achieving brahmanic Identity. What he thinks he becomes. The mind dilates infinitely and immerses itself in *Brahman* . . . (537).

Jñāna-yoga or the *yoga* of Knowledge is the most difficult path; many people have only an intellectual view of it without, however, reaching Realization (538).

The danger of *Vedānta-yoga* or *Jñāna-yoga* consists in dwelling only upon conceptual cognition. When Truth, unveiled by intuitive discernment, is not integrated in the context of individuality in such a way as to produce the integral transformation of the being, one falls into sterile and useless erudition. It is not sufficient to know that our body is a transitory compound of molecules, one *must really* consider it as such.

Yoga implies curbing thought movement; a *yogi* stops the flow of his thought completely and tries to make a white page of his mind. A *jñāna-yogi*, during meditation, has no care of his mental substance . . . He rests in *Brahman* by means of *brahma kara-vṛtti*, the vibration produced by listening to sacred formulae like this one: *Tat tvam asi* (That thou art) or *Aham brahmāsmi* (I am *Brahman*).

This *brahmakāra-vṛtti* constitutes a *sattva* modification. A *jñāni* remains a silent witness to mental modifications (he does not stop the *vṛttis* like the other *yogis*) and he uses the body and the mind as tools. He is always in *samādhi,* even when he acts, while other *yogis* are unable to enter *samādhi* unless they enter a closed room or assume a *yoga* position. The latter when in the waking state and when not in *samādhi* are conditioned by *māyā,* while the *jñāni,* on the contrary, does not need to assume a position nor does he need a closed environment, he is always in *samādhi* even when walking. A *yogi* in *samādhi* cannot work, while the *jñāni* can because he possesses a double state of consciousness, like a person who is trained to type or play the piano, or a woman who can knit or embroider while speaking with people around her.

For the *jñāni* there is neither trance nor absence of trance; he is always in *samādhi. Māyā* does not condition him.

There is, however, a difference at the beginning between *Yoga* and *Vedānta.* A *rāja-yogi* begins with the reason and the will cleared or, more exactly, he begins with *jīvātman.* The *jñāna-yogi* reasons, discusses, reflects deeply, analyses, synthesizes, discriminates, perceives spiritually. He adopts the negative way: *neti, neti* (not this, not this), I am not the body, I am not the mind; I am *sat, cit, ānanda* (pure existence, pure consciousness, pure bliss), I am *Brahman.* What he thinks he becomes.

A *rāja-yogi* converts all his *vṛttis* (thought movements) into a sole *vṛtti: samādhi* with mental attributes, and when he abandons this last trace of thought he enters into *nirvikalpa-samādhi* where all intellectual movement vanishes, thus realizing *Brahman*. A *jñāni* reaches *mukti* (Liberation) instantly; on the contrary a *rāja-yogi* goes through different stages, passing from one centre (*cakra*) to another, thus raising himself up gradually (539).

It is stated that a Realized *jñāni* is a Liberated One with open eyes, that is, even in his physical consciousness he remains as *ātman*, his own true Essence.

The theory of perception, as intended by *Vedānta* – writes Nityabodhānanda – has three distinct degrees: sensible perception, interpretation and consciousness. The *jñāni* is beyond these three degrees . . . The *jñāni* perceives things but 'sees God everywhere'. This simple phrase contains a profound truth: objects change, sensible knowledge varies and mental relations are joyous or joyless, but the *jñāni* observes all things with equanimity of vision.

The *Gītā* indicates this important concept in *sūtras* 24 and 25 of chapter XIV: 'The *jñāni* looks at mud and gold, at friends and enemies, at heat and cold, at praise and blame with the same eye'; this means that the *jñāni* in a flash goes through the three stages of sensible perception, of interpretation and knowledge. Where we have to proceed slowly he flies in an instant.

If I see a stone and a diamond, at once I enter into the plane of interpretation and I evaluate them: the first is of no use to me, the second can bring me a fortune; however, if I arrive at the plane of pure ideation, which is deeper than that of evaluation, the stones are of the same essence and importance; the idea of the stone is worth that of the diamond, and the duality between the two disappears. This is the plane of Knowledge where evaluating interpretation has no value . . .

The idea that I have today of God and the one that I had twenty years ago seem different, but they have the same nature. It is my reaction that is no longer the same, and the reaction is a temporal modality. Time brings modification to our perception, it transforms perception into knowledge and knowledge into ego.

The stable mind of the *jñāni* does not perceive oppositions; events are inscribed within the sphere of pure Knowledge and become identical; they are only mental objects, phenomena of the wakeful state.

The metamorphosis carried out by time is not necessary to the *jñāni*'s perception, while it is to ours. This is the difference between his interpretation and ours. The process of interpretation occurs between perception and knowledge; to interpret, two functions are indispensable: emotion and intellect. Let us give an example: we lose a friend and our emotional reaction is very strong. The emotional function is reawakened by the feelings and the attachment we feel for the departed person. Emotion, if not fully satisfied, brings us to the intellect, the function of which is to stabilize experience. Intellect transposes such experience into the cognitive sphere.

Interpretation is carried out in time with the help of the mind, as its nature is temporal.

For the *jñāni,* time is not necessary to knowledge, his perception is immediate (*aparokṣa*) as he determines himself as *ātman*. This knowledge is bared of the characteristics of our particular experience: objects and thoughts. When the *jñāni* is active upon the plane of *ātman*, the mind (with thought) – which is a projection of *ātman* – does not come into existence. If he has no mind, all the more he will have no preferences, evaluations and satisfactions: attributes, these, of the mind. This does not mean that the *jñāni* is devoid of emotions. His emotions are found sublimated into pure will: they cannot produce tensions nor do they contract out of fear of losing something.

As in the case of attention without an object knowledge is identical with consciousness, thus, for the *jñāni,* emotion is identical with intuition.

This comprehension frees the emotions and the intellect, so that they function simultaneously and immediately. In our case, on the contrary, reactions occur with some delay, prolonging emotions more than is necessary. Our tears are not participation in an unhappy event, but a personal reaction to that event . . .

The *jñāni* rejects the mind as an instrument of cognitive appropriation, because he has understood its deforming character. During meditation we force ourselves to achieve the arrest of all those interpretative activities in order to allow the mind to be absorbed by *ātman*. As long as we are possessed by the thought 'I am meditating', we are unable to meditate correctly because a thought like this, produced by the mind, means that the mind has not yet been 'absorbed'. When, on the contrary, we feel the Divinity working in and for us, then the state of meditation has been reached and the mind has disappeared.

For the *jñāni* the vision always remains identical, because the Divinity resides in all things, including the perceiving person, but this is difficult to understand.

We can consider an objective reality pervaded by the Divine, but how can we arrive at an intrinsic, subjective reality of the Divine? To claim to be able to see God as an object certainly constitutes lack of comprehension because, if it is true that God is this reality, He cannot appear as a simple concept but reveals himself in the ceasing of all experience and in the non-production of any thought.

His subjective Reality is not 'knowable'. When I speak to you, for example, the objectivity of this fact is not demonstrable; the event can be objectivated only through memory. Thus, the concept 'It is I, Mr X, who is speaking' does not place before us any demonstrable subjective reality. If instead I reflect 'It is I, Mr X, who is speaking' our dialogue ceases, giving way to my reflection. Where then does the subjective reality of he who speaks lie? If the subject no longer objectivates, we can say that the object is, as it were, in him and, in fact, one and the same thing as himself. We must seek the origin of the contradiction in our experiences. The mind considers experience as possession of an objective fact, but that very same mind tells us that there is a subjective reality behind that possession; it has a natural inclination to objectify, but the only possession which is possible to accomplish is that of memory.

If the mind is disappointed it turns towards its source, towards the Self, but once again it is not gratified because it discovers that the Self does not

> permit to be taken or grasped. We can note that the mind alone is responsible for our frustrations, in all and every kind of experience; it would be the case to abandon it, but without it experience loses all its consistency. On the one hand it states the reality of the experience itself and, on the other, it makes us discover the irreality of what we believed to be real. The best we can do is not attempt the impossible and admit the relativity of experience without seeking to kill the mind; we can consider this as a step towards the real Self, leaving to the a *ātman* the task of absorbing it.

Observing the last three methods described we may add that the *bhakta* overcomes the 'world' out of love for the Divinity, the *rāja-yogi* overcomes it because he dominates or transcends it, the *jñāni* ('seer', literally 'he who possesses Knowledge') overcomes it because he has understood and recognized it to be non-real in absolute terms. But, as we can notice, the aim is that of transcending the existing.

'My Kingdom is not of this world . . . They are not of this world as I am not of this world,' says Jesus.

[1] Svāmi Śivānanda, *Jñāna-yoga*. Editions Albin Michel, Paris 1949; Svāmi Nityabodhānanda, *Le chemin de la perfection selon le Yoga Vedānta*. La Colombe, Paris 1960.

9

Asparśa-yoga

'Man' (according to Meyerson) 'does metaphysics just as easily as he breathes, without thinking.'

The spontaneous need to set goals which are always beyond Man's fleeting dimension is part of human nature. Metaphysics was born with the cosmos itself, because every particle of the universe tends towards its total existential reintegration.

Man is a restless being and has always tried to go beyond his own natural condition, to conquer an after-life, often difficult to define, but which actually represents the refusal of every limitation and, therefore, negation of the composite and finite world of appearances.

'The secret of the method,' says Descartes, 'consists in seeking in everything, with great care, the absolute which is in it.'

The search for the Absolute is uppermost in Man's mind and implies that in all orders of reality there must be a Prime (*adhi*) term which is the condition of all the rest – and, as such, independent, at least within the limits of its own order – and which, in the more appropriate acceptance of the term, may be considered absolute and the only absolute, without any second.

It can be noticed that the philosophy (especially modern and western philosophy) which contests Man's ability to discover the Absolute, merely transfers the character of absoluteness into the world of sensible perception.

The metaphysician walks the straight road of integral awareness and of cognitive reintegration into the absolute Being from which all comes and emanates. Rather than taking an interest in the phenomenal and structural world, he aims at the absolute Being, or Non-Being, at the Undifferentiated, the Ineffable, the Unknowable (for the senses).

Metaphysics is interested in what is 'beyond physics', beyond nature, beyond gross, subtle and causal forms, beyond the substantial, beyond the very same One-Principle, beyond the God-Person, beyond all possible polarity. This implies that metaphysics is about the Absolute, the Constant, the Infinite, about Non-Being as pure and sole being, the Unconditioned, the One-without-a-Second (*advaita*). Metaphysics goes beyond the physical, the psychic, the spiritual. All that regards the individual and therefore the general refers to science; all that regards the universal, the transcendental unity, totality, refers to metaphysics.

If metaphysics is the quest for the Absolute and for Reality without a second then it cannot be conceptualized or fitted into certain individualized mental frameworks. The Absolute, or supreme Reality, cannot be circumscribed, represented or placed upon the plane of empirical relativism, nor can it be considered the exclusive property of any individual or people.

To achieve metaphysical realization, one must without doubt have specific qualifications, in particular a mind capable of synthesis and of a-temporal understanding. Many individuals are subjugated to time-space-causality and, indeed, it is difficult to emerge from it. But if one wishes to realize metaphysical knowledge, one must *fly*, one must take oneself beyond time and space, beyond the contingent, the individual, beyond the general; in other words, one must be able to remain *without supports*. From this comes the name *asparśa* which means non-contact, without relations, links and supports. From this comes also the proper kind of attention which must be given to it, as this is a special and particular type of knowledge which does not operate in a manner in keeping with commonly used discursive or empirical knowledge. It is the true 'Way of Fire', because it burns all *māyā*'s objectivating possibilities and because the entity unveils and demonstrates itself in its self-splendour. To grasp a-temporality directly means not to base oneself upon any type of practical *yoga* or psycho-physical exercise; it means sinking abruptly into the all-containing and all-pervading Present. Metaphysical realization can be achieved by that particular kind of mind which we might call *mens informalis*.

This metaphysical *yoga* was presented by Gauḍapāda and by Śaṁkara, the two great masters of *Advaita Vedānta*.

Gauḍapāda states in his *Kārikās*:

> I bow to this *yoga* – taught by the Scriptures themselves – well-known as *asparśa*, free from relations, beneficial, generator of bliss for all beings, devoid of oppositions and of contradictions.
>
> *Māṇḍūkyakārikā*: IV, 2

'*Asparśa-yoga*,' comments the great Śaṁkara, 'is the *yoga* without *sparśa*, contact or relations whatsoever; it belongs to the nature of *Brahman* (*nirguṇa*). The knowers of *Brahman* call it by this name; in other words, it is called *asparśa*, that *yoga* free from all (causal) relations. It becomes a blessing for all beings. Some aspects of *yoga*, austerity (*tapas*) for example, are associated with suffering, although they are said to bring about intense happiness; but this *yoga* does not belong to similar categories. What then is its nature? It is bliss for all beings.

We can say that the enjoyment of a particular kind of object may bring happiness, but not constant well-being [enjoyment of any order or degree is always dual, therefore conflictual]; *Asparśa-yoga,* on the other hand, brings bliss and at the same time stable well-being because its nature is beyond impermanence. Besides, it is devoid of oppositions. Why? Because it is devoid of contradictions. To this *yoga,* taught by the Scriptures, I pay my homage.'

> This *yoga,* which is called *asparśa* (without any contact), is difficult for many *yogis* to understand, because those who feel the fear (of annihilation) where it does not exist, are afraid of it.
>
> *Māṇḍūkyakārikā*: III, 39

'*Asparśa yoga namā*: this is known,' comments Śaṁkara again, 'as *asparśa yoga, yoga* without contact-support, as it has no relations (with anything), it is not, therefore, in contact with anything. It is described in the *Upaniṣads.* A *yoga* of such a kind is hard to be attained by *yogis* lacking in true knowledge of the *Upaniṣads.* The idea is that this Truth can be realized only as a consequence of a thrust, the crowning of which is awareness of *ātman* as the sole Reality (without-a-second). The *yogis* fear (this kind of *yoga*) while they should not be afraid of it. The non-discriminating ones fear, by practising this *yoga,* the extinction of their individuality, even though (*asparśa*) is beyond all fear.'

The term *asparśa-yoga* seems a contradiction in that *asparśa* means 'without contact' and *yoga* means 'contact, union of two things'. The first word refers to what is devoid of relations, which implies absolute non-duality which cannot have any kind of contact with things, because from the point of view of the ultimate truth there cannot be anything else but the Absolute in its indeterminateness. The second term implies relations and contact between two things: the created and the Creator, the individual *jīva* and *Īśvara,* the individual and the universal consciousness, and so on.

Gauḍapāda, to the road that leads to the Absolute, to the One-without-a-second, to *nirguṇa Brahman,* gives the name of *yoga,* meaning 'method', which can eliminate the obstacles which prevent the Truth from revealing itself.

> The knowledge of the illuminated being, which is all-pervading, has no relations with any object; thus the souls too have no relationship with objects . . .
>
> *Māṇḍūkyakārikā*: IV, 99

This reveals the way in which Knowledge (*Brahman*), which is all-pervading, has no connection with objects which are but mental representations. *Brahman* is not born, free from differences, without any second. Thus, *Asparśa-yoga* sets out on the pathway which leads directly to the realization of the absolute, transcendental Being. Its point of view is of a pure metaphysical order because its flight points directly to the non-dual Principle without descending into the realm of duality. It is the authentic 'Philosophy of Being' in that it is pure and sole Being.

Grasping absoluteness is difficult because the mind, which operates within the realm of subject-object, cannot understand the absolute non-duality. Those who strive to place the Absolute within the framework of simple mental representation struggle in vain. One may safely say that this *yoga* requires an approach of Identity. In other words, as it is a *yoga* without relations it is obviously a *yoga* without supports. Thus it requires an immediate entry into the Self, without the help of either external objects or qualifications of the individuality itself such as feeling, will or empirical knowledge.

The other kinds of *yoga* all require a vertical thrust, an impulse which stems from individuality in that it is an effect, and which directs itself towards its own transcendence; therefore they require desire. On the pure metaphysical pathway the determining factor is no longer desire, but the very awareness of the fact of 'finding oneself', of *being*. The disciple is not pushed forward, but held back; one might well say that he is not driven towards the acquisition of anything inferior or superior but towards the solution of all *māyā*'s instances, including that of Union as it is commonly understood.

The *Asparśa-yoga* disciple withdraws into himself

and apprehends the Absolute, which unfolds in all its majesty within the secret core of his own heart. Beyond all ideas, concepts, ideals, idols, phenomena, there is *That* which is Totality not subject to or depending upon any concept or change. The 'Metaphysical Reintegrated One' has the virtue and the privilege of seeing all the phenomena of life in the light of the metaphysical Zero.

Asparśa-yoga leads to active reintegration and realizes that one Essence which is not differentiated, which is uncreated: that a-causal, non-manifest and impersonal state from which every universe-object emerged as a chain of perceptions of *māyā*'s light.

Being *is*, and there is nothing more to be added, because to say that Being is 'this or that' means that that Being *is not*. Again, to say that it may be different from what it is means stating that a datum *is* and at the same time *is not*. Besides, if Being has 'become' this or that, then it must have come from a Being or from a non-being. If it comes from a non-being then the absurd is stated because from nothing, nothing is produced; if it comes from Being, then we must agree that Being stems from Being, which means that it remains identical to itself in its indivisibility and, in this case, there can be no talk of 'becoming' or of 'birth' or of finding oneself in another condition because Being which remains identical to itself does not undergo any movement, birth, or change.

What is required is a certain type of understanding, not of the sensible order, and to consider that what is universal, absolute, a-formal cannot be transposed into a particular dialectical perspective, nor into a dogmatic, rational set of concepts. The metaphysical pathway stands upon the plane of informal intelligence so that the emotional sphere is completely excluded from it.

This type of *yoga* is that of pure insight into things or appearances; it goes beyond all kinds of phenomenology, all common reason, all religion, all changing social moral and sensible experience, as these things are all the fruit of mediated knowledge. Metaphysical truths cannot be closed into schemes, concepts or mental analytical frameworks, because they transcend all physical experience. On the other hand, to meditate on what does not correspond to any sensible-formal datum is not easy; the sensible mind needs to conceive reality in relation to forms and images, and often the image itself captures the thinker who should be, in fact, independent. The metaphysical pathway presents some difficulties because one must abandon the normal thinking process and accept conditions that permit uncommon, a-formal, a-dimensional understanding. It requires abandonment of the personal and collective unconsciousness.

A premature approach to this kind of pathway might paralyse the normal process of sensible perception and thought without achieving access to or the possibility of superior understanding. The outcome would be mental inertia and boundless confusion, with aberrant states of consciousness leading to the annihilation of the mental dynamics. This danger may become acute in the West where the tendency is more towards a sensible-formal type of mind that, moreover, is considered unique and irreplaceable.

The metaphysical pathway is certainly one which apprehends the Infinite with all its virtual possibilities of manifestation and manifested; but this *understanding* is integral Realization, in that the adept achieves effective, conscious, non-theoretical Identity (otherwise knowledge would only be erudition); nor is this Identity virtual because this condition has always existed and has never been lacking. One does not arrive at *Asparśa-yoga* by means of self-imposed discipline nor through faith nor by means of devotion or by any action set off by individual-sensible expression, but by means of deep, inner self-awareness, so that all extroverted energetic motion tends to fade away, because the *spirit* is completely free. Once the undivided Point is reached, the notion of translatory movement no longer exists; the *spirit*, having eliminated the form or extinguished the reflection, enters into its own essence, devoid of cause, time and space.

Asparśa-yoga represents the last step and the goal of all human experience and realizative possibility. Beyond all experience there is the 'moment' of total comprehension of our very essence; it is the culmination of perfect equilibrium and of the pre-existential a-condition. The common individual is bound to the concepts of time and space, therefore to the manifest, to the evolving object; only a few are able to unveil the *eternal present*, the Alpha and Omega of what is commonly called change. The metaphysician, not satisfied with having known and transcended the limited realm of subject-object, dares to climb up to the last a-formal step of the universal vibratory stairway to discover himself.

Asparśa-yoga may be considered as being the highest expression of spiritual knowledge, that comprehension which leads from the unreal to the Real, from death to Life, from the finite to the Infinite, from the relative (human and divine) to unqualified Absolute without a second, from illusory differentiation to supreme Identity.

10

Realization and Psychological Comfort

Many people approach *yoga* initiatory schools and organizations, seeking realization or liberation, but only a few have a clear idea of the implications

Those who devote themselves to such spiritual research should first of all ask themselves what they are really looking for, what *yoga* or Realization may ask of them, and then examine which group, organization or instructor may be best suited to their particular aim.

Some think that Realization must lead to a greater expansion of the empirical self; people say that someone has 'realized' himself because he has satisfied most of his egoical needs. Thus, an individual of financial, political, artistic or cultural fame is considered as a 'realized' one. In this case the meaning and value of Realization are completely reversed.

Others believe that the mere fact of belonging to a church, an esoteric or *yoga* group implies the right to sit 'at the table of the Gods', even opposing the rest of humanity.

Others still believe that by following a group, a Master or a *guru* in a strict and fanatical manner they have already reached the 'opposite bank', or that they have crossed the 'great abyss'.

Then there are the self-taught ones who cannot bear to have a guide or an instructor, who submerge themselves in books and become highly erudite, and then consider themselves to be initiated, even Masters, capable of guiding souls on the awakening.

These categories of people (and many more) are obviously of a profane nature; they have little or nothing to do with aspiration towards the 'Sacred' because they display the basic error into which they have fallen.

There is also a category of aspirants to spiritual research which undoubtedly 'aspire' in a sincere and innocent way, but which are still a prey to *rajas* – energies at various levels. They are dispersive people; they turn to this and that in order to satisfy their manasic needs, they go from one *guru* to another; they undertake journeys in the belief that Truth, Realization or Liberation are to be found outside of them; however, they are in good faith.

Then there are those who attend a group for years,

but who assume a passive attitude, without becoming active, self-aware and well-directed disciples, so that the whole group is obliged to drag them along almost bodily. Others still, although their intentions are good, are limited by a fairly heavy *karma* which stresses them and deprives them of energy.

Others have an excessively emotional approach and behaviour, with all the consequences that this dual energy brings with it.

There are neophytes who seek a Master with great emphasis, but who are just looking for a confirmation of their own ways, and when this does not occur, they can react badly. The ego always wants gratification and consent. Others arrive at a form of 'bribery': they practise *yoga* or follow the way of spirituality on condition that they obtain health, economic or professional prosperity, a good marriage (if one wishes to form a family), the resolution of family conflicts and so on, and all this with conscious and unconscious motivations.

We shall not speak of those who know exactly what they want, where and for whom to look; they do not need stimuli, nor words; they are already prepared and well-directed.

But what does Realization really mean? Who must realize? What does Liberation mean, and from what must we strive to free ourselves? What does being an Initiated One mean?

There are many today, for example, who practise

yoga, but what does practising *yoga* really mean? What does *yoga* demand of us? What types of *yoga* are there?

A good aspirant, postulant or novice should inform himself and acquire at least a minimum view of the various spiritual currents so as not to find himself one day deeply disappointed, so as not to waste precious energies, and start having a proper relationship with Realization.

To answer these questions we must begin by looking at what the constitution of the entity or person is in its totality, according to the *yoga,* initiatory and even religious vision, otherwise certain concepts will always remain vague and unclear. This is all the more valid in the case of typically western people or western 'consciousness', which may not have a clear vision of words, concepts or events that are beyond their cultural ken. The West has been a long time imbued with councillary Christian doctrines whose values are peculiarly religious and whose contents are: The God-Person or the Father, grace, faith, sin, penitence, obedience, sacraments, Creator-created duality, the devil, hell, salvation, Jesus Christ and so on. These are key concepts from which not even the atheist or the materialist is totally free, even though he may think he is.

Concepts such as Realization or Liberation go beyond the western view and most people cannot avoid comparing them to the religious dimension.

Some eastern Masters speak of Knowledge also

as a means of Liberation, but this vision too is alien to western religious thinking because for the Catholic Christian the means of salvation are faith, good deeds and grace, while for the Protestant faith alone is sufficient.

We have given these few indications so as to show how, very often, one may approach things about which one does not entirely know the implications.

Now, taking up the topic just mentioned, we can state that all the initiatory Traditions of the East and of the West assert that the entity is the synthesis of Spirit, Soul and Body (to speak in religious terms, see St. Paul); of *noûs, psyché* and *sôma*, according to the Ancient Greek Tradition; of *ātman, jīvātman* and *ahaṁkāra* to speak in *Vedānta* terms. We could mention others, but the principles would remain the same; only the names would change.

The *noûs-ātman* is the divine spark in us, it is of the nature of the supreme Being; the *psyché-jīvātman* is the Soul or the mediator between pure Spirit and *sôma;* finally, the *ahaṁkāra* represents the objective part of the entity, the ego-body-*sôma*. Such principles or states of consciousness, insofar as they can express themselves on all levels of existence, have a spatial reference point of their own, a particular influence upon certain vital spheres.

At this point we must also mention, according to the sole universal initiatory Tradition (because in actual fact there is really only one Tradition with different branches which adapt to the needs of different peoples), the various existential spheres upon which the life of the entity unfolds. We shall take into consideration the *Vedānta* vision.[1]

Ātman is beyond time-space-cause, it is the pure metaphysical 'state' of the entity; the *jīvātman* works principally upon two existential planes; *brahmaloka* and *hiraṇyaloka*; the *ahaṁkāra* (the principle of individualization) operates upon the levels of *manavaloka, kāmaloka* and *pṛthivīloka*.

Brahmaloka (*loka* = place, state, dwelling) is the dwelling-place of *Brahmā*, of the Being-Person, of the God of the entire manifested world; *hiraṇyaloka* is the place of the consciential state of the Gods, it is the intelligible world; the *manavaloka* corresponds to the third 'heaven' of which St Paul speaks and is characterized by the thought process, but we find ourselves already in an individualized state, even if it is the highest one which individualization can reach; the *kāmaloka* is the place or state of consciousness of unfulfilled desires, of passions; the *pṛthivīloka* is the sphere of the earth, of the corporeal plane, of the gross level which we know through the five senses, while the other planes are super-physical or subtle.

According to the qualities (*guṇas*) they express, the entities direct themselves towards this or that sphere, so that their way will be *devayāṇa* or *pitṛyāṇa*.

We can illustrate this by the following diagram:

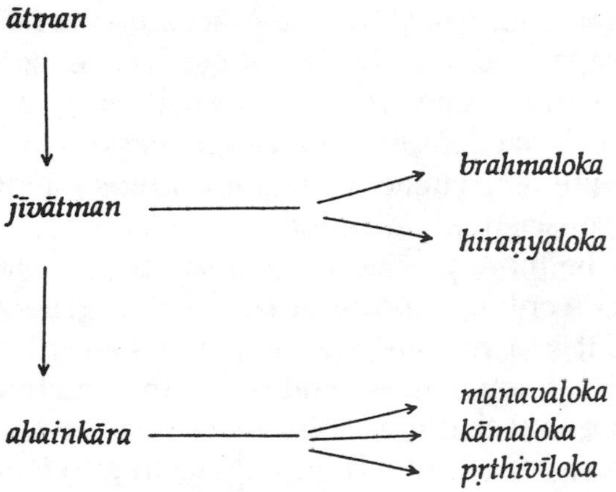

Manas and *kāma* can be put together because where one is to be found the other is there too; one usually speaks of *kāma-manas* to express the mental-sensible state.

Having posed the problem, in order to understand what Realization-Liberation implies and what it requires of us we should understand another very important thing, which is the basis and the very aim of the realization process.

If we speak of Realization or Liberation, there is something in us that is not realized, which is not completed or which is held in thrall. Therefore, we must try to understand what it is in us that is enslaved or in a state of unfulfilment.

Let us say that the *jīvātman-soul-psiché* is a simple consciential reflection of the a-temporal *ātman*, and that *ahaṁkāra* is, in turn, a consciential reflection of the *jīvātman*. *Ahaṁkāra,* the reflection of a reflection, has separated itself from and has weakened its contact with the universal counterpart, thus becoming particularized, individualized, believing itself to be absolute when in actual fact it is merely a reflection of a consciential reflection.

To be more precise we can say that *ahaṁkāra,* as such, is only the 'sense of ego', 'what generates the ego', it is a reference-point; it is when it identifies with a body-vehicle and with the qualities that belong to it that it expresses itself as 'I am this and not another'. *Asmitā* (I am), according to Patañjali's *Rāja-yoga,* is identity or the fusion of consciousness with the power of knowing or with the qualities belonging to the vehicle-bodies of manifestation.

When this occurs we have one 'I am this' in opposition to another 'I am this', with consequent oblivion of the divine counterpart. In this context a separation takes place; the umbilical cord is 'slackened' to such an extent as to create a separate individuality. With individualization we have the triumph of *I am I* and *you are you;* I am this body and you are that body which is different from mine; in other words we have made an appearance absolute.

The various religions speak of the 'fall': the Christian religion tells us that we are fallen Angels; Adam, by eating the fruit of the tree of good and evil, 'fell' into the I-you dualism; Plato speaks of the 'fall' of the Soul into generation wherefore it is necessary to give it back its wings and make it fly towards the world of the intelligible which is its true homeland.

'My kingdom is not of this world,' says Jesus. *Vedānta* says that *ahaṁkāra*, the reflection of the *jīva*-soul, completely identifies, as we have seen, with its expressive body-vehicles and therefore with individualized qualities, thus forgetting its universal-intelligible origins.

We might go on quoting other Traditions, but as we have said before, this would mean changing only the names or the concepts, and the substance would remain the same. We are speaking, of course, of pure initiatory Traditions.

The reader that has followed us to this point will understand the meaning of Liberation or Realization. Realization implies resolving a separation; Liberation implies freeing oneself from what, as pure consciousness, one is not. *Yoga,* and here we mean any kind of *yoga,* means *union,* joining; it is therefore necessary to unite what has been separated.

We are of the same Essence as the supreme Being in that It *is* and does not become, but by an act of free will we identify with becoming, forgetting our divine nature: it is the myth of Narcissus who, falling in love with his 'shadow' or 'reflection' thrown upon the water, falls and 'dies' to his previous consciential state. However, nobody prevents us from returning to our original condition. The difficulties are represented only by the *degree of identification* which we have achieved with our 'shadow', with what appears and disappears, with changing phenomena, with *māyā,* as *Vedānta* would put it.

It is obvious that to go back to one's true original state implies returning within oneself until one finds Consciousness without a second, beyond all objectual identification (instincts, emotions, thoughts are all objective data which may be observed, manipulated, dominated and transcended).

According to Plato one must *remember* what one really is. The Soul which has fallen into oblivion of itself must reawaken, according to the splendid image that he gave of the charioteer who has fallen asleep and of the chariot with two horses, one white and one black, which are also alchemical symbols.

We are beings, or better still, *universal consciousness,* inclusive and all-pervading, and we should recover our nature by dissolving that second artificial and illusory nature which we have made for ourselves (the nature of the 'shadow') and which caused us to disregard our divine origin. This identification with our second nature is so strong in the majority of us that it is difficult, almost impossible, to prospect the first. We can say that the majority of people are alienated and it cannot but be so.

All those who approach some kind of *yoga,* initiatory School, self-realization Philosophy and so on without knowing these things and without trying to bridge the gap, are either in good faith or mystifiers.

An authentic Initiated is a person who has found a way to fill the gap, to reverse the 'fall' and transcend his second nature until he has re-established *unity*; an Initiated is one who has found the way to extract gold from his cave, as the alchemical expression goes and make it shine in all its splendour.

Individualization reveals itself through assertion of the self as a separate 'I', through pride, 'desire' to be desired, loved, through various kinds of passion, the instincts of the form, and so on.

An Initiated who is worthy of that name, a Freed, a Realized One no longer has any of these characteristics; we can safely say that – and we do not think that this will create 'scandal' in the western aspirant – He no longer has *got any human qualities* because He is something more; in fact, at certain levels he is pure *ātman* outside of time-space and cause, therefore beyond becoming and all form of duality; He is one-without-a-second.

An authentic Realized is 'his own lamp' in that he is Self. He does not need anything because he has quenched all those desires that belong to the 'shadow'. He lives of 'self-propulsion'. He is a Sun that rotates upon its own axis giving off 'light' and 'heat'. A desire of any kind or intensity whatsoever is an unfulfilled thing; it is a want, it is lacking, and these things belong to that 'shadow' precisely because it *is not*.

We gave the title 'psychological comfort' to this chapter: why? Because very many people seek only psychological comfort, a way of occupying their time, a means for spending time with others who do things out of the ordinary, a way of resolving conflicts and tensions that have built up within the family or at work; there are, in fact, some western and eastern *gurus* who favour this kind of choice, thus helping to perpetuate the separate individuality so that it can possibly express itself with less tension. These are therapeutists, psychologists. Other *gurus* even help people to develop latent psychic powers to satisfy their vanity and compensate their psychological frustrations. In brief, all these things are carried out within the sphere of individualized psyche so as to maintain and perpetuate that empirical *psychological ego* which acts upon the sensible plane, and not in order to transcend it and resolve it in the ontological Self.

On the other hand, at all times, individualization leads to conflict, pain and alienation, and there is no policy, economy, erudition or empirical science that can give fulfilment, peace, serenity and bliss to an alienated and fragmented consciousness. Individuality, therefore, or the fruit of the 'fall', is synonymous with pain-suffering (see the four noble Truths of Buddha, which are the very bases of Buddhism), so that this individuality, rather than try to resolve and transcend itself, seeks only digression from its wants and its incompleteness.

In fact, when the prospect of transcending the ego with all its products is proposed and one tries to carry out Realization positively and practically, one can notice that individuality runs away. As long as this individuality or this illusory second nature simply goes to conferences and listens to words, or satisfies itself with reading, with *yoga* postures or singing, it accepts, gratifies itself and comforts itself, but when consciousness is nailed down to return within itself by means of adequate techniques or processes, then comes the moment of refusal.

The majority do not seek 'initiatory death' but, paradoxically, seek to escape conflict while at the same time wishing to remain in conflict. The majority seek psychological comfort in order to 'survive' and protract their 'I am this' until the end of the incarnation. The majority seek outside of themselves what is within them, according to the indications of the great Initiated Ones, including Jesus; the majority want to be freed from the pain they suffer while continuing to promote the causes that produce that sufferings. The majority, in brief, want to be comforted.

Individuality is hungry for comfort, it wants to be accepted, desired, satisfied and gratified because, in reality, *it is not*; and as it is not an absolute reality it can never be happy and fulfilled, no matter how much one may give to it. And so it passes from one yearning to another, from one request to the next, from one event to another, without finding relief.

Often the majority let go, resign themselves and invent all kinds of sophisms to convince themselves and others that life is like this, that the world works this way, that one must take it for what it is. This is a reductive, masochistic view of things and means refusing to solve the problem of one's incompleteness. Thus the world is full of conflict, pain, cruelty and aberration of all kinds because people want it to be so, because we do not try to change the philosophy of the world, because we do not want to lose a part of us that lives on illusory projections, because we are content with the compensatory crumbs which, instead of solving the problem, only complicate it or put it off.

Spirituality, in its most ample sense, is often the source of compensation and comfort for those consciousnesses which are not prepared to face the 'monster' which dwells within them. Even 'charity work' may prove to be an innocuous source of compensation or of psychological comfort; the action of a disciple may prove to be dual, it may always turn out to have a compensatory component.

Many are pressed by a heavy *karma*, by lack of harmony and by psychic disturbances wherefore they are desperately looking for help and comfort; if they do not get it they rebel. In our day family 'warmth', as well as the sense of friendship, is gone, and even rest and physical relaxation are rare, because everyone is committed to material gain in order to meet the needs dictated by the alienating consumer malady. Not only does this rat race not lead to Being, it also dehumanizes, even brutalizes people, creating greater alienation and leading to conflict of all kinds and, paradoxically, to graver uncertainty.

Others enrol in initiatory schools for reasons of prestige, for ambition, to acquire titles, offices, grades and functions; again, for psychological compensation. And to all these seekers of 'worldly values', to all these misfits, to these resigned people, certain *gurus,* both East and West, offer *comfort;* some even offer a hedonistic type of community-society of the *carpe diem* variety, permitting a placid licentiousness that borders libertinism, so as to dull themselves and forget the natural privations of individuality. In other words they prospect the Biblical 'golden calf'.

Let us say in all sincerity that most Hindu and Buddhist *yoga* methods operating in the West offer only therapeutical motives, so that the Christian and the non-believer can easily classify them as methods for gratifying the selfish ego, for feeling better and for self-expansion.

The fact is that Realization, Liberation or being true Initiated requires precise qualifications; in other words, *one must be ready.* If there is no specific *vocation,* no deep *calling* of the consciousness, and not of the 'beggar ego', a burning for the things that *are* and which do not become, there can be no talk of *yoga,* of Realization, of Liberation, and not even of Salvation in the Christian sense. If there is no precise instance for the supra-sensible then it would be better not to undertake the process of realization or of initiation to avoid coming up against sure disappointment, which will only prove to be a further source of conflict, and in order to avoid desecrating what little Sacredness desperately strives to resist this *Kali-yuga*.

Realization as such brings its own fruit which is, according to the univocal indications of two great and authentic Masters, Plato and Śaṁkara, stable Bliss and stable Knowledge. However, many prefer that conflict which derives from unstable and contingent sensible enjoyment.

Authentic and resolutive Knowledge is directed towards all – there are no privileged ones or predestined persons – even if not all are prepared to accept it and *live* it; therefore It can be given only to a few (compared to the millions of 'sleeping ones') who, having been bitten by the serpent of bitter *avidyā,* have woken up to the awareness that something is wrong within them.

Our wish is that all may find Bliss by following the pathway best suited to their particular needs (whether it be eastern or western is of little importance as long as it is a pure Pathway), because everybody contains within himself that immeasurable treasure which, due to an act of *identification* with what is fleeting and perishable, he has forgotten completely.

Our wish is that all may put back wings on their Soul which is relatively fallen, and take flight towards the supreme peaks of Bliss-without-object, our true nature which, although 'darkened' or veiled, can never be destroyed.

[1] In the texts published by Edizioni Āśram Vidyā one may find the correlations existing between this and other Traditional branches: *Orphism, Platonism, Qabbālāh, Alchemy*.